Laura Brown is:

a) An award-winning writer and editor

b) Extremely fond of oysters

c) An erstwhile teen magazine agony aunt

d) @EnchantedTrifle on X

e) All of the above

Sian Meades-Williams is:

a) An award-winning writer and editor

b) A pistachio ice cream fan

c) Founder of media industry newsletter
Freelance Writing Jobs

d) @SianySianySiany on X

e) All of the above

Answer to both: e

THE FEMINIST QUIZ BOOK

Questions That Celebrate Iconic Women Through Time

BLINK
bringing you closer

First published in the UK by Blink Publishing
An imprint of The Zaffre Publishing Group
A Bonnier Books UK company
4th Floor, Victoria House
Bloomsbury Square,
London, WC1B 4DA
England

Owned by Bonnier Books
Sveavägen 56, Stockholm, Sweden

facebook.com/blinkpublishing
twitter.com/blinkpublishing

Hardback – 978-1-788703-56-7
Paperback – 978-1-785121-57-9
Ebook – 978-1-788703-57-4

A CIP catalogue of this book is available from the British Library.

Designed by IDSUK (Data Connection) Ltd
Printed and bound in Great Britain by Clays Ltd, Elcograf S.p.A.

1 3 5 7 9 10 8 6 4 2

All answers correct as of December 2023

Blink Publishing is an imprint of Bonnier Books UK
www.bonnierbooks.co.uk

To excellent women everywhere

CONTENTS

Foreword by Sara Pascoe   ix

Welcome to *The Feminist Quiz Book!*   1
Literature   5
Geography   17
Mathematics   29
Drama   39
Science   53
Politics   63
Art and Design   77
Music   91
Physical Education   103
History   117

Answers   131
Report Card   203
Further Reading   207
Acknowledgements   215
Image Credits   217

FOREWORD BY SARA PASCOE

Gosh, I love a quiz! It's where competitiveness and being a know-it-all meet. Footballers might score once or twice a match (if they're lucky). A quizzer will feel that sublime rush of achievement several times a round. There's the satisfaction of knowing something and buzzing in with absolute certainty because you studied Jane Eyre at school or read an article on Napoleon Bonaparte last week. Such smugness, such unadulterated pride. Even more enjoyable than that is the answer which emerges from the mist. Looming elusively, half-remembered, tip-of-the-tongue – 'Ssh, ssh, everyone, let me think. . .who *was* the second man on the moon?' Just as you give up, Buzz Aldrin hits your brain like lightning, and you snatch the pen with adrenaline pumping and no manners. Answer scribbled, you lean back with arms folded, all is well in your intellectual kingdom. But nothing beats a correct guess. A plucked-from-the-air, baseless, clueless guess. 'I dunno when Ted Heath was Prime Minister, it was before I was born, 1979? I dunno, write 1970. No, 1960! No, 1970.' When your knowledge-less conjecture is pronounced

EXACTLY RIGHT, your self-confidence does a victory lap, high-fiving angels as you wonder 'Maybe I *am* a genius . . . should I get my A-levels remarked?!'

While there's much delight in knowing and point-scoring, I believe the most pleasurable part of a quiz is the learning.

'Ooooh, I had no idea Louis Theroux was Justin Theroux's cousin!' 'I can't believe cucumbers can be used as pen erasers!' 'I didn't know that Google was originally named *Backrub*!'

Like going for a run makes you fitter, every quiz leaves you a little bit cleverer. It's a knowledge explosion, and when it's over, you mentally tidy all the new dates, names and places away neatly and hope you'll be able to find them again when you need them.

That's why *The Feminist Quiz Book* is such a good idea – you can show off how much you *do* know while simultaneously discovering brilliant women that you should have heard of but haven't. It's something I have to brush up on as much as anyone.

A couple of years ago, I was invited to perform stand-up comedy for Ada Lovelace Day*. The name sounded familiar, but rather than do any research, I trusted my assumption that Ada Lovelace was the name

---

* Research the date now as it IS coming up later!

of a high-street retailer of fancy knickers and sex toys. 'This is bound to be a *saucy* gig,' I thought as I prepared my material, 'I bet the audience will be screeching ladies wearing leopard print and furry handcuffs'. My set list included jokes about padded bras, spicing up a relationship and a routine about pornography. Sure, it was a bit weird to hold this event at the Science Museum, but I didn't appreciate my mistake until after my tumbleweed accompanied, ill-judged set.

Turns out Ada Lovelace wasn't Ann Summers, but a mathematician. Her input to computer science was as vital as my jokes were inappropriate. The organiser kindly filled me in as I sipped a consolatory wine. Ada Lovelace was Lord Byron's daughter; her mother had encouraged her to pursue maths so that she didn't follow in her dad's philandering footsteps. Ada's exceptional ability led to her working alongside Charles Babbage on his Analytical Engine. Her notes are described as 'visionary' and she's believed to be the first person who saw the potential for the engine to act upon more than numbers. The Analytical Engine is the world's first computer and thanks to an algorithm scribbled alongside an article, Ada Lovelace is the world's first computer programmer.

I was sad to be hearing about Ada for the first time. Mainly because I'd just told a roomful of science professors and PhD students my feelings on Wonderbras. But

I also wondered if perhaps I'd known more about the fascinating, gifted women in technology and maths, I would've been more interested in those subjects myself? You'll already be aware that many kids experience residual sexism in their education: 'boys are better at sums and angles while girls excel at sewing their feelings onto blankets'. But many teachers are working to improve this, hence the existence of Ada Lovelace Day, a celebration of women in Science, Technology, Engineering and Mathematics (STEM) for me to come along and ruin.

The under-represented need representation. As Billie Jean King told us, 'You have to see it, to be it'. How different will the ambitions and career expectations of young women be when they are taught of female achievements in equal measure with men? When they know that the entire world of knowledge is open and waiting for their study, and every intellectual mountain can be conquered if they choose?

Billie Jean King was pressured into playing a male tennis player in a 1973 match known as 'Battle of the Sexes'. She beat her opponent (I can't remember his name*) and gained respect and recognition for female athletes. But women shouldn't have to compete with men to achieve those things – feminism is not a contest, it's working on the creation of a level playing field (although if you *are* doing these quizzes with your brothers, I hope you thrash them). No one is trying to argue the women in this book are better than men, but they need their own space to be noticed at all. They deserve these pages.

Wanting to know more about Virginia Woolf and Ada Lovelace does not mean obscuring the genius of Charles Dickens and Isaac Newton. It actually gives us a better understanding of *all* the people whose brainy creativity our civilisation was built upon. Our world was shaped by all who preceded us, the technology we currently enjoy was a team effort. That's something of which we can all be proud. Even though we *personally* didn't do any of it.

So, sit down comfortably, with pen in hand, ready to eviscerate your opponents or to simply test your own knowledge in *The Feminist Quiz Book*.

* Joke! It was Bobby Riggs. Three points to me.

WELCOME TO THE FEMINIST QUIZ BOOK!

The Feminist Quiz Book brings together a collection of over 100 questions to test your feminist knowledge. Challenge your friends and family on what they really know, and delve into the fascinating history of women who refused, dared, led, questioned and discovered.

From coffee filters to electric refrigerators, find out what you know about Melitta Bentz and Florence Parpart – just two of the many women who created items that we use every single day. Discover the women who weren't afraid to be the first: Sojourner Truth, while fighting for the right to reclaim her son from slave ownership, was the first African-American woman to win a lawsuit against a white man in the United States; Jeanne Baret, the first woman to circumnavigate the globe; Mae Jemison, the first black woman to go into space. Test yourself on the women who have fought and keep fighting, dreaming and working to make the world a better place.

The chapters are split into different subjects and we'll tell you all about Mary Shelley and Leonora

Carrington, Rosa Parks and Simone Biles, while taking you on a journey through history, art, literature, drama, music, sports and myriad other subjects that have been shaped by dozens of women that you wish you'd learned about in school.

THE RULES

Aside from not sticking your chewing gum under the table, there really are no rules. There's no homework. There's no detention. And you can wear whatever colour shoes you like. How you read and engage with this book is entirely up to you. You'll find a mix of easy, middling and difficult questions to test your knowledge, with one, two or three points next to each question. If, like us, you were the nerdy one in class and you enjoyed tests and getting your marks at the end of the lesson, there is a scoresheet at the back.

You can also pick and choose a chapter that takes your fancy – maybe you want to brush up on your science smarts or you don't know much about female artists. Whichever order you complete the questions in, the answers start on page 131.

Our favourite way to go through the book is picking a question at random and reading it out loud to whoever happens to be nearby: your mum, dad, sister, brother, partner, housemate, the stranger next to you on the bus or even your cat!

Whichever way you play, we hope that you have fun and learn a little something about these brave and astonishing women who broke the rules and changed the world. Women who, in so many cases, risked their lives to do something, when so many people told them they couldn't. If you've been inspired by the women we've included in this book – and there were hundreds more we could have mentioned – there's a reading list at the back so you can find out more about their lives.

May all the women in your life be given the opportunity to excel.

LITERATURE

If you are holding this book in your hands, then congratulations! You have excellent taste in books and, undoubtedly, women.

For many of us, reading books is how we make sense of our thoughts and the world around us. And, indeed, so is writing. It's how Elizabeth Barrett Browning counted the ways. It's how Sylvia Plath processed her feelings about her father and her husband. Writing, choosing the right words and phrases, is how Wendy Cope expressed how happy oranges make her, and how such small moments can encapsulate the joy of life.

Literature isn't just an expression of creativity, it's a way of recording the world. A way of saying, 'I was here, this happened to me, this is how it felt.' But you only have to flick through an issue of the *London Review of Books* or listen to the questions on *University Challenge* to know that women's writing still doesn't get the acknowledgement that it should. The word 'chick-lit' is whispered in hushed tones, as though women's lives and experiences aren't meaningful and don't hold value.

But here's the thing: while women's voices are vital, and we know that writing for oneself is of huge value, women's stories are also profitable. People buy them. In droves. Beatrix Potter was a self-made businesswoman. Virginia Woolf didn't just write her own books, she co-owned publishing house Hogarth Press, and E.L. James's books have sold over 150 million copies worldwide.

These voices are how we connect to one another – a shared book between friends, a voice note sent late at night or a snapshot of a passage we loved. Words move us. They change us. Whether it's a rabbit in a blue jacket or a particularly hot sex scene, in so many ways we are the collective sum of the books we read and the words we share. And frankly, we'll take reading the back of a shampoo bottle while we're in the shower over yet another literary novel where a male professor just can't help falling in love with one of his female students.

This chapter is all about the incredible women who have contributed to the literary landscape throughout the years and whether you are a reader or a writer, we hope their words inspire you.

1. **Who wrote, 'I would venture to guess that Anon, who wrote so many poems without signing them, was often a woman'? (1)**

   a) Virginia Woolf
   b) Gertrude Stein
   c) Rebecca Solnit

2. **Which 1900s Harlem Renaissance author was buried with no marker on her grave? (2)**

   _____

3. **Match the female writer to their male pseudonym. (1 point for each correct answer)**

Anne Brontë	Ellis Bell
Louisa May Alcott	Isak Dinesen
Mary Ann Evans	Currer Bell
Charlotte Brontë	Vernon Lee
Amantine Lucile Aurore Dupin	Acton Bell
Emily Brontë	A.M. Barnard
Violet Paget	James Tiptree Jr.
Karen Blixen	George Sand
Alice Bradley Sheldon	George Eliot

4. **What major event in Mary Shelley's life is said to have taken place on her mother's grave? (2)**

   a) She signed her first book contract
   b) She lost her virginity
   c) She celebrated her 21st birthday

5. **Which romance novelist began a scheme in the Second World War to ensure that war brides had a proper wedding dress to wear on their big day? (2)**

   a) Barbara Cartland
   b) Danielle Steel
   c) Catherine Cookson

6. **How many Booker Prize winners since the competition began in 1968 have been women? (2)**

   a) 27   b) 4   c) 18

7. **Of those winners, which two have won the prize twice? (1)**

8. **True or false? Margaret Wise Brown, author of *Goodnight Moon*, once threatened to kill a publisher with a bow and arrow. (2)**

   _____

9. **Crack the codes to name the authors of these books. (1 point for each correct answer)**

   EXAMPLE:
   TSTS, TBP, TNATG, ASH: Iris Murdoch (The Sea, The Sea, The Black Prince, The Nice and the Good, A Severed Head)

   a) WT, OB, NW, ST

   _____

   _____

   b) SOS, B, P, GHTC

   _____

   _____

c) TSOTB, TIM, HF, TSK

_____

_____

d) R, R, P, TMWMHJ

_____

_____

e) TJLC, TKGW, TBD, TVOA

_____

_____

f) HOAYS, A, PH, WSABF

_____

_____

g) TTV, TLS, F, TNW

_____

_____

10. Which author is believed to have coined the term 'dinner party'? (2)

_____

11. Which three things did Françoise Sagan, the author of *Bonjour Tristesse*, say were more amusing than knitting, housekeeping and one's savings? (2)

    a) Cheese, dancing and jazz
    b) Gin, writing and sex
    c) Whisky, Ferraris and gambling

12. Name the book from these first and last lines (there are clues to the number of letters in each word). (2 points for each correct answer)

First lines

It was a queer, sultry summer, the summer they electrocuted the Rosenbergs, and I didn't know what I was doing in New York. (3, 4, 3)

_____

There was no possibility of taking a walk that day. (4, 4)

_____

Last night I dreamt I went to Manderley again. (7)

_____

They shoot the white girl first. (8)

_____

Snowman wakes before dawn. (4, 3, 5)

_____

They say when trouble comes close ranks, and so the white people did. (4, 8, 3)

_____

'Christmas won't be Christmas without any presents.' (6, 5)

_____

The first place I can well remember was a large pleasant meadow with a pond of clear water in it. (5, 6)

_____

Miss Brooke had that kind of beauty which seems to be thrown into relief by poor dress. (11)

_____

You better not never tell nobody but God. (3, 5, 6)

_____

Last lines

He was soon borne away by the waves, and lost in darkness and distance. (12)

_____

An excellent year's progress. (7, 6, 5)

_____

But, in spite of these deficiencies, the wishes, the hopes, the confidence, the predictions of the small band of true friends who witnessed the ceremony, were fully answered in the perfect happiness of the union. (4)

_____

For there she was. (3, 8)

_____

'There was the hum of bees, and the musky odor of pinks filled the air.' (3, 9)

_____

'Are there any questions?' (3, 9, 4)

_____

GEOGRAPHY

At a time when women couldn't go out for dinner on their own, many of the women in this chapter had the courage to explore the world without a chaperone. The act of women crossing geographical boundaries is more than just about their position on a map – it's social, it's political. Many of these women dared to have no fixed destination and instead chose to wander aimlessly. Some of them traded in their good standing in society so they could see the world. Others had to dress as men just to keep safe and sometimes that wasn't precaution enough. Still they kept on putting one foot, one hoof, one wheel in front of the other. Their exploration paved the way for millions more adventurers. From Anne Lindbergh's solo flights and Bessie Coleman's stunts, to Aimée Crocker's adventures in Hawaii (where she was officially named an island princess) – today's wanderlust would look very different without these women taking the first steps.

Exploring the world may have been a pursuit traditionally reserved for men, but it's in our nature as humans: seeing what's over that hill (maybe a monster), discovering what's around that corner (could be Meg Ryan in a bookshop) or just trying something new because we can. Curiosity, wonder, excitement – they're all traits that weren't always encouraged in women, but that desire to know more about the world gives our lives purpose; it connects us as people and it makes us more open-minded about other cultures and communities, and for these women that was encouragement enough.

Every journey the women in this chapter embarked upon was daring. Sometimes dangerous, even life-threatening. The thing these women all have in common is that they shaped our view of the world. Crucially, their inspiring accounts give the lesser-explored parts of the world a fresh voice and perspective. The women who make up the questions in this chapter are proof that the length of the journey doesn't matter, it's what you discover along the way that's really important.

1. Which journalist and explorer travelled around
    the world in 72 days but still found the time
    to stop in Singapore and buy a monkey called
    McGinty? (1)

    a) Nellie Bly
    b) Martha Gellhorn
    c) Harriet Chalmers Adams

2. Jeanne Baret dressed as a man to join Louis-
    Antoine de Bougainville on his voyage in
    1766 and she became the first woman to
    circumnavigate the globe. The expedition was
    credited with the discovery of over 70 species.
    How many were named after her? (2)

    a) 35   b) 12   c) 0

3. Helen Thayer has trekked across the Gobi Desert
    and lived with a pack of wolves in the Arctic
    Circle. How old was she when she became the
    first woman to complete a solo expedition to the
    magnetic North Pole in 1988? (1)

    a) 27   b) 50   c) 18

4. **Complete the wordsearch to discover the women throughout history who have dressed themselves as men to explore the world. (1)**

Isabelle Eberhardt
Jeanne Baret
Isobel Gunn
Calamity Jane
Dervla Murphy
Lady Hester Stanhope

F	J	A	H	O	M	P	V	E	E	F	H	C	R	B	V	E	D
J	M	I	T	C	H	D	J	W	D	Q	D	X	J	K	D	P	E
P	Q	K	O	A	G	M	A	C	A	N	Y	E	C	V	T	O	R
L	T	U	B	W	U	L	M	J	G	Z	A	A	A	Y	C	H	V
Z	R	H	C	L	E	E	E	N	R	N	J	J	Y	L	P	N	L
Z	I	Y	L	A	K	N	S	S	N	W	L	U	N	C	D	A	A
I	S	A	B	E	L	L	E	E	B	E	R	H	A	R	D	T	M
L	C	H	P	N	G	A	B	H	U	G	H	K	T	T	P	S	U
U	G	M	N	P	A	A	M	L	U	G	O	I	S	Y	H	R	R
K	F	J	G	V	R	I	V	I	G	O	D	E	I	G	O	E	P
E	K	W	E	E	B	F	T	T	T	Y	R	H	R	V	V	T	H
G	Q	N	T	C	M	R	B	S	D	Y	A	Z	T	Z	F	S	Y
N	N	U	G	L	E	B	O	S	I	R	J	E	V	A	D	E	U
T	H	T	N	H	E	J	V	B	R	R	C	A	Q	K	U	H	L
Z	O	O	H	E	N	O	J	Y	I	D	H	N	N	K	E	Y	Z
M	U	V	J	K	M	P	T	N	Q	N	D	C	M	E	A	D	E
S	M	Q	U	I	R	J	T	J	Q	U	D	E	T	A	A	A	H
V	J	N	O	M	W	X	G	Q	E	V	M	E	X	N	W	L	X

5. **What beauty tool saved Evelyn Cheesman's life while she was exploring the jungles on the Colombian island of Gorgona? (2)**

   a) An eyelash curler
   b) A nail file
   c) A perfume atomiser

6. **Match the method of transport with the explorer. (1 point for each correct answer)**

Lady Hester Stanhope	Bicycle
Amelia Earhart	Motorcycle
Ellen MacArthur	Foot
Isabella Bird	Zeppelin
Mary Kingsley	Camel
Eva Dickson	Horse
Polly Letofsky	Canoe
Lady Grace Drummond-Hay	Aeroplane
Van Buren Sisters	Racing car
Annie Londonderry	Yacht

7. **True or false: Gertrude Bell's wardrobe for her 1913 trip to Arabia included silk underwear and 12 hats. (1)**

8. Namira Salim has skydived over Mount Everest and she's on course to become the first Pakistani woman to go into space. What other incredible achievement does the explorer have under her belt? (2)

_____

_____

9. What age was the youngest woman to climb Mount Everest when she reached the summit? (2)

    a) 16 years and three months
    b) 13 years and 11 months
    c) 19 years and seven months

10. Unscramble the names to discover the women who helped map the world. (2 points for each correct answer)

    MANY CREPES _ _ _ _ / _ _ _ _ _ _ (the UK's leading cartographer)

    HARM PIRATE _ _ _ _ _ / _ _ _ _ _ (mapped the floor of the ocean)

    PAPILLARY SHELLS _ _ _ _ _ _ _ / _ _ _ _ _ _ _ _ _ (creator of the London A–Z)

ABRASIVE HARKING _ _ _ _ / _ / _ _ _ _ _ _ _ _ _ _
(mapped the dark side of the moon)

EEL ONLY FRECKLE _ _ _ _ _ _ _ _ / _ _ _ _ _ _
(mapped Chicago's destitute areas in the late
19th century)

HANDSAW HI TIT _ _ _ _ _ _ _ _ _ _ _ _ _
(mapped the history of the Beothuk tribe in
Newfoundland from memory)

11. **What's the name of the American explorer who
become the first woman to travel to both the
North and South Poles? (2)**

a) Ann Bancroft
b) Sophia Loren
c) Meryl Streep

12. Identify which explorer said these inspiring
    quotes and use their names to fill in the
    crossword. (3)

ACROSS:

4 and 3 down. 'Someday I'm going to visit that land. And then I will write my own adventures.' (7, 8, 5)

8 and 11 down. 'Wouldn't it be better to die doing something interesting than to drop dead in an office and the last thing you see is someone you don't like?' (7, 7)

10 and 12 down. 'Why should I be a footnote to somebody else's life?' (6, 8)

13 and 8 down. 'Everything suggests a beyond.' (8, 4)

14 and 2 down. 'As soon as we left the ground, I knew I had to fly.' (6, 7)

17 and 9 down. 'We drop down or get run over, but we never retire.' (6, 8)

DOWN:

5 and 15 across. 'Indescribably fascinating, indescribably romantic.' (3, 7)

7 and 1 across. 'I hurried away with an unconquerable wish to see the world.' (3, 8)

16 and 6 across. And 'Where are the many women?' (6, 3)

MATHEMATICS

We don't often think of maths on its own. We do sums to work out if we can splurge on a takeaway two days before payday or to figure out our weekly shop, but we're far more focused on the end result – an extra portion of spring rolls, or the fancy bottle of wine – than we are the actual process. For most of us, our days of algebra and equations are largely over. So, perhaps it's understandable that mathematicians can sometimes be overlooked.

But maths is very often the precursor to something else and what it leads to is frequently groundbreaking. The maths that NASA's human computers worked out shot rockets to the moon, and an entirely different set of calculations landed them safely. The complex equations used in chemistry help us to discover elements and win Nobel Prizes. In the world of physics, maths leads to unquestionable breakthroughs in our understanding of the world. Mathematicians have created algorithms that impact every element of our daily lives, even though we may not realise it.

Female mathematicians didn't always make the headlines but without the work of the women in this chapter, those big moments might never have happened. Alan Turing might not have solved Enigma during the Second World War. The *Apollo 11* mission might not have been a success. We might have taken much longer to discover planets in our solar system. The accomplishments of the women in this round are much more than the sum of their parts and their achievements stand on their own.

1. **When is Ada Lovelace Day? (1)**

   a) The third Wednesday in June

   b) The first Saturday in April

   c) The second Tuesday in October

2. **Cryptanalyst Joan Clarke is best known for her work as a codebreaker at Bletchley Park. She worked alongside (and was also engaged to) Alan Turing and helped crack the Enigma code. What was unusual about her academic qualification from Cambridge University? (3)**

   a) Her double first qualification wasn't listed on her degree certificate

   b) Her name was spelled incorrectly

   c) She was denied her full degree

3. **In a letter to *The New York Times*, Albert Einstein wrote of a fellow mathematician that they were 'the most significant creative mathematical genius thus far produced since the higher education of women began'. Who was he writing about? (2)**

   a) Emmy Noether

   b) Hypatia

   c) Maria Gaetana Agnesi

4. **Match the mathematicians and computer scientists to the space project that they helped make a reality. (2 points for each correct answer)**

Margaret Hamilton	Cassini
Annie J. Easley	Project Apollo
Melba Roy	The Viking Program
Barbara Paulson	SCOUT Launch Vehicle Program
Dorothy Vaughan	Project Echo

5. **Which mathematician and scientist features on a Scottish £10 note? (1)**

   a) Mary Somerville
   b) Flora Philip
   c) Sheila Scott Macintyre

6. **Reorganise these events in the order they happened. (3)**

   a) Maryam Mirzakhani, the first Iranian mathematician to win the prestigious Fields Medal, dies of breast cancer, aged 40.
   b) Mary Everest Boole published the book *Philosophy and Fun of Algebra* for children. Her

creative methods changed the way maths was
taught in schools.

c) Karen Uhlenbeck became the first woman to
win the Abel Prize, often referred to as the
'Nobel Prize for Maths'.

d) Russian mathematician and women's rights
advocate Sofya Kovalevskaya was born.

e) Mary Jackson became NASA's first African-
American female engineer.

7. **Sophie Germain's theory of elasticity was used to
create which tower? (1)**

a) The Eiffel Tower
b) The Blackpool Tower
c) The Leaning Tower of Pisa

8. **Maria Gaetana Agnesi was the first woman to
write a mathematical handbook in 1748. Why did
she give up her career as a mathematician? (2)**

a) She devoted her life to helping the poor
b) She decided to travel around the world
c) She got married and had several children

THE FEMINIST QUIZ BOOK

9. **Which well-known nurse also became a pioneer in the field of applied statistics by collecting significant amounts of patient data? (1)**

   a) Edith Cavell
   b) Clara Barton
   c) Florence Nightingale

10. **Answer these questions in numbers. (3 points for each correct answer)**

    a) In what year was Hypatia – regarded as the first female mathematician – murdered?

    _____

    b) How many siblings and half-siblings did Maria Gaetana Agnesi have?

    _____

    c) Katherine Johnson helped calculate *Apollo 11*'s trajectory to the moon. How many miles per hour was the spaceship travelling?

    _____

d) The famous photograph of Margaret Hamilton (below) shows her next to a huge stack of paper containing the code for new space computer software. Approximately, how many pages are in the computer programme?

DRAMA

For a significant period of theatre's history, it was illegal for women to act professionally on stage. Some of the greatest roles for women – Lady Macbeth, Olivia, Desdemona – were played by men.

We could say that things have moved on since then, but that wouldn't be strictly true. Sexism and exploitation have been rife in Hollywood since the silent movie era, with women treated as commodities and loaned out from studio to studio. Actresses and performers were locked into contracts and forced to play roles they didn't want to. The #MeToo movement that shook – and is still shaking – the entertainment industry today is only just the start of things changing.

Director Alice Guy-Blaché made the first-ever narrative film, *La Fée aux Choux* (*The Cabbage Fairy*), in 1896 and went on to make over 1,000 more. Yet an American newspaper still wrote a story about her with the headline 'Charming Little Woman Runs Movie Business with Success'. When silent film actress Lois Weber stepped behind the camera, she pointed her lens at gritty topics no one else was making films about, such as abortion and birth control. Ida Lupino's films also focused on hard-hitting women's issues. But these women never did become household names; their films weren't seen as important. Now, women behind the camera have to fight to get their films seen – especially women of colour. In 2020, there were no women nominated for Best Director at the Oscars, despite there being a plethora of films that year directed by women which had received critical and commercial acclaim.

For everyone who says that people don't want to watch films made by women, about women's experiences, refer them to Reese Witherspoon, who took her Hollywood career into her own hands and launched her production company, Hello Sunshine. Her first film, *Wild*, earned her an Oscar nomination. Her second, *Gone Girl* – based on Gillian Flynn's bestselling novel – grossed $369.3 million worldwide. These aren't just side hustles or passion projects, they're multi-million-pound ventures.

From Natalie Portman who wore a dress to the 2020 Oscars with the names of female film directors embroidered into it, to the 16 black actresses who took to the Cannes Film Festival in 2018 making the powerful statement '*Noire N'est Pas Mon Métier*' ('Black Is Not My Profession'), women across Hollywood are speaking up.

But it's not just about the huge films and megabucks. As filmgoers, we want to see characters from similar backgrounds – small towns, council flats and countries around the world. We all want to watch people who are like us and be inspired by women telling women's stories and sharing their experiences. Seeing those experiences amplified to audiences all around the world is why culture is so important.

1. Only three films directed by a woman have won an Academy Award for Best Director (yes, it really does bring into question the whole Hollywood awards system). Name these films and their directors. (3)

_____

2. Actress Hedy Lamarr was promoted by her film studio Metro-Goldwyn-Mayer (MGM) as 'The Most Beautiful Woman in the World', but alongside her Hollywood career she was also a keen inventor and held patents for several inventions. She created a piece of technology that evolved into something we still rely on today. What was it? (2)

a) A microwave
b) Wireless technology
c) The first mobile phone

3. What year were women finally allowed to act on stage in England? (2)

a) 1560 b) 1660 c) 1760

4. **Unjumble the anagrams to discover the groundbreaking actresses. (1 point for each correct answer)**

    RAYS DIDO _ _ _ _ _ / _ _ _

    JEDI FOOTERS _ _ _ _ _ / _ _ _ _ _ _

    UNHARDY BURPEE _ _ _ _ _ _ / _ _ _ _ _ _ _

    VEILING HIVE _ _ _ _ _ _ / _ _ _ _ _

    NETTABLE CATCH _ _ _ _ / _ _ _ _ _ _ _ _ _

    HINTED PIPER _ _ _ _ _ / _ _ _ _ _ _

    RELAX COVEN _ _ _ _ _ _ _ / _ _ _

    GOPHERWOOD GLIB _ _ _ _ _ _ / _ _ _ _ _ _ _ _

    AIRWORTHY HAT _ _ _ _ / _ _ _ _ _ _ _ _

    CHERRIED AILMENT _ _ _ _ _ _ _ / _ _ _ _ _ _ _

    LAW COBRA _ _ _ _ _ / _ _ _

    BRAT AHEAD _ _ _ _ _ / _ _ _ _

    BRING DREAMING _ _ _ _ _ _ / _ _ _ _ _ _ _

    LACUNA BALLER _ _ _ _ _ _ / _ _ _ _ _ _

5. **Actresses Bette Davis and Joan Crawford's famous feud lasted for decades, how many films did the pair star in together? (1)**

6. **After successfully suing her film studio, which actress had a lawsuit named after her? (2)**

   a) Olivia de Havilland
   b) Joan Fontaine
   c) Vivien Leigh

7. **Match these women to the film industry firsts.**
    (1 point for each correct answer)

First black actress to win an Oscar	Zubeida Begum Dhanrajgir
First Chinese star in Hollywood	Fatma Begum
First female director of Indian cinema	Janet Gaynor
First black female film star	Helen Gibson
First named silent movie actress	Josephine Baker
First Best Actress Oscar winner	Hattie McDaniel
First female Hollywood stunt woman	Florence Lawrence
First Indian talkie actress	Anna May Wong

8. **Fill in the blanks to complete the names of these films directed by women. (1 point for each correct answer)**

a) _____ Wedding
b) _____ Bird
c) The _____ Fairy
d) Something's Gotta _____
e) The Trouble with _____
f) _____ Face
g) Fast Times at _____ High
h) Bend it Like _____

i)   Little _____

j)   A _____ of Their Own

k)   The _____ Suicides

l)   _____ Strength

m) Zero _____ Thirty

n)   A _____ in Time

o)   You've Got _____

p)   _____ Strong

9. **Tippi Hedren is best-known for starring roles in the Hitchcock films *Marnie* and *The Birds*. She also kept an unusual dangerous animal as a pet. What was the animal? (1)**

a) A crocodile called Andrew

b) A king cobra called Dave

c) A lion called Neil

10. **Edith Head won a record eight Oscars throughout her costume design career – she's actually won more Academy Awards than any other woman. Name the films from these pictures of her iconic designs. (1 point for each correct answer)**

a)

b)

c)

d)

e)

f)

SCIENCE

We've all heard of Albert Einstein, Charles Darwin and Edwin Hubble. Even if we don't quite know the ins and outs of their work, we know their names. Naming women scientists is another matter entirely.

Perhaps more than any other chapter in this book, the connections between the works of different people are crucial. One discovery leads to another, and then another, and another. These discoveries can influence research happening across the world. One disproven theory can clear the path for a significant breakthrough, a piece of seemingly insignificant data in one research paper can be the final piece of a puzzle for another experiment. The world of science is collective, and much stronger for it. And, of course, that includes knowledge and discoveries made by women.

Women helped get us to the moon. Women have helped detect and cure cancers. Women have discovered different species all over the world. Their discoveries have helped others to expand our collective knowledge in such magnificent ways that we cannot even begin to imagine what will come next.

No single element completes our understanding of the universe, but a significant amount of the puzzle pieces are groundbreaking discoveries by women.

Despite this, women often saw credit for their work go to their male peers. Some women scientists didn't even have access to the equipment they really needed to do their jobs, simply because they were women. So they did without. And boy, did they *excel* at their jobs. Gertrude B. Elion's work in medicine led to breakthrough drugs for AIDS and leukaemia. Jewish Italian Rita Levi-Montalcini was kicked out of the University of Turin after Mussolini published his 1938 *Manifesto of Race*, but this didn't stop her – her work with nerve growth cells led to a Nobel Prize in 1986.

There has always been a gender gap in the sciences. It's decreased significantly, but it's one that still can't be ignored. Recent UCAS figures show that of students studying core STEM subjects, just 35% of them are women. While the number of women in the science professions is growing, the imbalance is still there. That imbalance impacts all of us.

In this chapter we're celebrating the women we didn't learn about in science classes. We're uncovering the incredible discoveries they made that changed all of our lives. So put on your safety goggles and get ready to meet some of the world's finest scientific minds.

1. **Williamina Fleming, Annie Jump Cannon and Henrietta Swan Leavitt were just some of the 80 women in the not-so-charmingly named 'Pickering's Harem'. What did they do? (2)**

   a) They were all astronomers
   b) They were all chemists
   c) They were all biologists

2. **Match the scientific achievement made by the women Edward Pickering hired (while each being paid the princely sum of 25–50 cents per hour, half what men would have been paid). (2 points for each correct answer)**

Discovered the Horsehead Nebula	Antonia Maury
Classified over 350,000 stars	Cecilia Payne-Gaposchkin
Determined the sun's chemical composition	Henrietta Swan Leavitt
Calculated the distances of stars from Earth	Annie Jump Cannon
The first woman astronomer to publish a star catalogue	Williamina Fleming

3. **Who was the first person to be awarded two Nobel Prizes? (1)**

   a) Marie Curie   b) Irene Curie   c) Lise Meitner

4. **What groundbreaking discovery did Lise Meitner play a key role in? (3)**

   a) Radiation   b) Nuclear fission   c) Black holes

5. **Mae Jemison was the first black woman to go into space. What year was her space flight? (2)**

   a) 1972   b) 1982   c) 1992

6. **Fill in the missing vowels to complete the discovery made by women. (1 point for each correct answer)**

   a) Rh_n_ _ m
   b) P_l_n_ _ m
   c) R_d_ _ m
   d) K_vl_r
   e) DN_ Str_ct_r_
   f) BRC_ G_n_
   g) D_rk M_tt_r
   h) R_d_ _ P_ls_rs
   i) N_cl_ _ r Sh_ll

7. The Nobel Prize has been awarded to just
   25 women in science. How many can you name?
   (1 point for each correct answer)

   _____

   _____

   _____

   _____

   _____

   _____

8. Who were the Edinburgh Seven? Can you
   name any of them? (2, plus 1 point for each
   you can name)

   a) The first group of women to study medicine at
      university
   b) A Victorian women's group who enjoyed
      writing science-themed detective stories
   c) An MI6 group who planted codes in science
      journals

9. In the 1690s, pioneering German naturalist Maria Sibylla Merian divorced her husband and then took her daughter on a trip to Suriname in South America, where her scientific studies and illustrations of insects illuminated the entomology world. In 2018, a rare insect was named after her. What was the insect? (1)

   a) Earwig   b) Butterfly   c) Dragonfly

10. Mary Anning was a palaeontologist living in Dorset who changed our understanding of the Jurassic era. Among her many fossil discoveries in Lyme Regis were the first complete ichthyosaur and plesiosaur as well as the dimorphodon. What popular verses were written about her? (1)

   a) The tongue twister 'She Sells Seashells on the Seashore'
   b) The Beatles' song 'Octopus's Garden'
   c) The nursery rhyme 'Mary, Mary, Quite Contrary'

'DON'T LET ANYONE ROB YOU OF YOUR IMAGINATION, YOUR CREATIVITY, OR YOUR CURIOSITY. IT'S YOUR PLACE IN THE WORLD... MAKE IT THE LIFE YOU WANT TO LIVE.'

MAE JEMISON

POLITICS

In 1918, women were finally given the right to vote in the UK. It marked a hard-fought victory for the suffragettes, whose battle had begun in 1832 when Mary Smith from Yorkshire petitioned her MP that women should 'have a voice in the election of Members [of Parliament]'. Decades of imprisonment, hunger strikes, death and destruction followed.

The Representation of the People Act only allowed women over 30 who met certain criteria to vote. Around 22% of women who were old enough to vote couldn't do so because they didn't own or rent property – or weren't married to a man who did. The suffragettes' campaign was far from over, and it took another 10 years until women in the UK were granted the exact same voting rights as men.

Around the world, similar fights were taking place, and many had already been won. Finland, New Zealand, the Isle of Man and Australia were among the first places to allow some women to vote (though many Indigenous Australian women – and men – couldn't vote until 1965).

Other countries took a lot longer to bring about much-needed reform. Women in Switzerland couldn't vote until 1971, with one region denying them the right until 1991. Saudi Arabian women voted for the first time in 2015.

Once the right to vote was secured, many women could also become politicians in their homelands – but it would be a long time before we got our first female leader. In 1960, Sri Lanka's Sirimavo Bandaranaike became the first woman to be elected as head of government in the modern world. She was soon followed by India's Indira Gandhi and Israel's Golda Meir.

Women's voices are still woefully lacking in most countries even now, and only around a quarter of the world's politicians are women. Men are still making decisions on everything from abortion bills and domestic abuse laws to equal pay disputes and maternity rights. Every woman who stands for election, runs for leader of her country and fights for the good of her people is also taking a vital step towards greater parity in politics.

This round comes with a disclaimer. Politics is a ruthless and divisive beast, and some of these women have chequered histories and held questionable views. There are some dames in these pages that you'll loathe, and others you'll adore. But in a world where the most powerful country on the planet can be run by a reality TV star, all these women have a place in the history books – even if we don't always agree with their politics. In the words of Beyoncé: 'Who run the world? Girls.'

1. What nationality was the first woman to take up her seat in the House of Commons? (1)

   _____

2. True or false? Suffragette Sophia Duleep Singh was Queen Victoria's lady-in-waiting. (1)

   _____

3. Match the women to their political catchphrases. (1 point for each correct answer)

Love trumps hate	Jacinda Ardern
Unbought and unbossed	Pussy Riot
¡No pasarán!	Shirley Chisholm
When they go low, we go high	Lady Hale
Let's do this	Hillary Clinton
Women are equal to everything	Emmeline Pankhurst
Deeds, not words	Michelle Obama

4. On 5 October 1789, the Women's March on Versailles took place. It became a defining moment of the French Revolution, but what were the women protesting against? (2)

   a) Wine rationing
   b) A ban on making cheese
   c) Bread shortages

5. **The names of these political leaders, past and present, have been jumbled up. Can you unscramble them? (1 point for each correct answer)**

COURTESAN LINGO _ _ _ _ _ _ _ / _ _ _ _ _ _ _ _ _
(Scotland)

A GLEAM KERNEL _ _ _ _ _ _ / _ _ _ _ _ _ (Germany)

A DRAIN HIDING _ _ _ _ _ _ / _ _ _ _ _ _ (India)

ABOARD KNIT SKIRT JOT _ _ _ _ _ _ /
_ _ _ _ _ _ _ _ _ _ _ _ (Iceland)

TEETERED KNIFE MRS _ _ _ _ _ / _ _ _ _ _ _ _ _ _ _ _
(Denmark)

AREA THYMES _ _ _ _ _ _ _ / _ _ _ (United Kingdom)

6. **Which country has the highest percentage of women parliamentarians? (2)**

   a) Rwanda   b) Cuba   c) Bolivia

7. **She's often referred to simply as AOC – but what is this American politician's full name? (1)**

   _____

8. **Hidden in the grid are eight genuine reasons that male MPs gave, in the run-up to the Representation of the People Act being passed, for why women shouldn't be allowed the vote. Can you find them all without angrily throwing something across the room? (2)**

Deadly logic	Too controlling
Female intuition	Men's responsibility
Enormous hats	Falling birth rate
Gusts of sentiment	Lack of judgment

Q	D	Y	X	I	T	T	U	M	L	L	U	J	L	B	W	E	F
M	E	N	S	R	E	S	P	O	N	S	I	B	I	L	I	T	Y
E	V	N	O	I	T	I	U	T	N	I	E	L	A	M	E	F	L
T	L	E	O	P	C	A	E	S	D	N	O	R	P	Q	V	U	D
A	O	E	N	R	E	N	B	I	S	G	T	S	Z	O	H	E	C
R	G	A	C	K	M	R	U	E	Y	V	B	U	F	D	Y	I	L
H	J	T	O	O	C	O	N	T	R	O	L	L	I	N	G	L	E
T	U	S	W	H	E	F	U	T	A	H	V	F	P	O	N	A	S
R	Z	A	P	G	G	E	R	S	C	K	U	J	L	I	X	U	S
I	T	R	H	A	M	G	Y	W	H	E	I	Y	B	T	Q	R	U
B	M	J	O	B	Q	M	F	K	M	A	L	E	V	U	T	A	H
G	D	A	I	Y	E	E	S	A	E	D	T	L	I	N	G	C	Z
N	W	I	F	X	R	N	K	C	A	H	R	S	G	W	O	I	Q
I	T	N	E	M	I	T	N	E	S	F	O	S	T	S	U	G	C
L	N	G	V	A	Y	I	D	J	L	P	S	G	K	X	S	U	I
L	E	S	P	L	A	C	K	O	F	J	U	D	G	M	E	N	T
A	Y	E	B	D	R	E	T	P	G	K	P	C	T	O	N	C	S
F	E	M	A	P	S	A	R	W	U	X	I	O	H	L	D	G	J

9. Can you identify these women protesting for better workers' rights? (3 points for each correct answer)

a)

_____

b)

_____

c)

d)

e)

10. **In 2019, Stella Creasy made history by becoming the first female MP to do what? (1)**

    a) Breastfeed a baby in the House of Commons
    b) Appoint someone to cover her maternity leave
    c) Claim statutory maternity pay

11. **What was the difference between suffragists and suffragettes? (1)**

_____

'TREMENDOUS AMOUNTS OF TALENT ARE LOST TO OUR SOCIETY JUST BECAUSE THAT TALENT WEARS A SKIRT.'

SHIRLEY CHISHOLM

ART AND DESIGN

'We don't embroider cushions here.'

That was architect Le Corbusier's response to furniture designer Charlotte Perriand when she applied to work at his atelier. A few weeks later, he saw her work at an exhibition and hired her on the spot. From that moment on, he took credit for many of her designs.

Her experience is shared by so many other women in the design industry. Men have just about accepted that women can design clothes, textiles, ceramics and jewellery – often dismissing these highly skilled disciplines as 'crafts' – but when it comes to cars, buildings and gadgets, there's still a 'just leave it to the guys, sweetheart' attitude to be found.

Many women have been written out of the design history books, but the problem of equality and fair-recognition rumbles on today. Research conducted by the Design Council in 2018 exposed that only 22% of the UK's professional designers are women, even though they make up 63% of students on creative arts and design courses at universities.

Likewise, the *Teenage Mutant Ninja Turtles* have made it easy for even the most art-averse among us to rattle off the names of four male artists without thinking – sometimes even via the medium of song – but the same can't be said for the *grandes dames* of art.

Many have been sidelined by the art world, society and the men in their lives. They've been relegated to the ranks of wife, sister, friend, muse. Galleries certainly aren't overflowing with pieces by female artists: 74% of fine art students are women, but 96.1% of artworks sold at auction are by men. It won't surprise you to learn that many women artists in the past have had their work misattributed and their achievements overshadowed by male artists. No one knew that Swedish artist Hilma af Klint was probably the first abstract painter in the world until 1986, for example.

Some artworks, including one by Dutch Golden Age painter Judith Leyster, even had their signatures painted over by dealers in order to sell more easily. We've heard more than enough about art created by men, and it's usually accompanied by a cacophony of trumpet-tooting and willie-waving. It's time to celebrate the incredible women of the art and design world.

1. **Cipe Pineles was one of Condé Nast's most prolific and pioneering graphic designers and art directors, and she became the first female member of the Art Directors' Club of New York in 1943. Can you solve these clues to find the magazines she worked on? (1 point for each correct answer)**

   a) Glitz and . . .

   _____

   b) The age you can become a blood donor in the UK

   _____

   c) The French word for Miss

   _____

   d) Third time's a . . .

   _____

   e) Let your body move to the music

   _____

   f) Becky Sharp is this novel's protagonist

   _____

2. **What unusual dish did surrealist painter Leonora Carrington once serve up to her friends? (2)**

    a) An omelette made from their own hair
    b) Clay and cheese sandwiches
    c) A bowl of deep-fried house flies

3. **Guess the fashion designers from their trademarks. (2 points for each correct answer)**

    a) Pirate boots

    _____

    b) Wrap dresses

    _____

    c) Slogan tees

    _____

    d) Miniskirts

    _____

    e) Avant-garde silhouettes

    _____

    f) Wedding dresses

    _____

4. **Unscramble these brilliant architects. (2 points for each correct answer)**

WAND JEER _ _ _ _ / _ _ _ _

BARONIAL BID _ _ _ _ / _ _ / _ _ _ _ _

A HARMONY MIFFING IRON

_ _ _ _ _ _ / _ _ _ _ _ _ / _ _ _ _ _ _ _

A BEELINE REVENGE LORRY

_ _ _ _ _ _ _ / _ _ _ _ _ _ _ / _ _ _ _ _ _

MANORIAL JUG _ _ _ _ _ / _ _ _ _ _ _

5. **Elizabeth Magie created an early version of which popular board game? (1)**

a) Guess Who?   b) Ludo   c) Monopoly

6. **Where did Georgia O'Keeffe prefer to paint? (2)**

a) In her car
b) In her water bed
c) In her swimming pool

7. **Can you match these textile designers to their patterns? (3 points for each correct answer)**

Anni Albers
Orla Kiely
Lucienne Day
Astrid Sampe

a)

b)

c)

d)

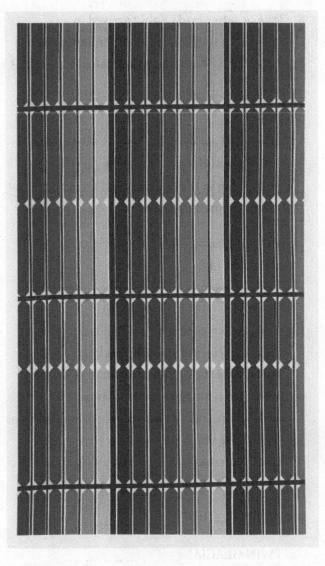

8. True or false? Frida Kahlo arrived in an ambulance to the opening of the first solo exhibition of her work in her native Mexico. (2)

_____

9. Edmonia Lewis was the first woman of African-American and Native American heritage to make it big in the international art scene. What was her chosen discipline?

   a) Photography
   b) Sculpture
   c) Embroidery

10. Our offices would look very different without the achievements of Shirley Jackson. In 1973, she became the first black woman to achieve a PhD from Massachusetts Institute of Technology (MIT). Unscramble these anagrams to discover the inventions that were made possible thanks to her research with subatomic particles. (1 point for each correct answer)

   AXMAN CHIEF _ _ _ / _ _ _ _ _ _ _

   TWIN GLACIAL _ _ _ _ / _ _ _ _ _ _ _

HOPE TO LUNCHEONETTE _ _ _ _ _ - _ _ _ _ /

_ _ _ _ _ _ _ _ _

SPIFLICATE COBBER _ _ _ _ _ - _ _ _ _ _ / _ _ _ _ _ _

ACE DRILL _ _ _ _ _ _ / _ _

11. **Match the inventor with their brilliant food-based invention. (1 point for each correct answer)**

Carmela Vitale	Ice cream maker
Agnes Marshall	Paper coffee filters
Melitta Bentz	Pizza saver
Florence Parpart	Chocolate chip cookie
Ruth Graves Wakefield	Electric refrigerator

'WHEN A WOMAN BECOMES HER OWN BEST FRIEND LIFE IS EASIER.'

DIANE VON FURSTENBERG

MUSIC

Although our record collections and Spotify playlists are overflowing with wonderful songs by women, the reality is that inequality is rife in the industry. The facts and figures might surprise you – this is an issue that goes far deeper than #GrammysSoMale or a bloke-heavy BRIT Awards.

In America, women performed less than a quarter of the 600 most popular songs from 2012 to 2017 – and only 12% of the writers of said songs were female. Behind the scenes, just 2% of producers are women.

The situation in the UK isn't any better – in fact, it's getting worse. In 2008, 35 of the 100 most popular songs that year were credited solely to women. A decade later, the number had shrunk to just 13. Collaborations have also become more commonplace, and that means Man feat. A Different Man and Maybe Even Another Man are saturating the charts, so there are now three times as many guys than gals making the country's favourite music. What's more, only 19.6% of artists signed to UK record labels are women.

Away from the charts, festival organisers are still being lambasted for their blinkered lack of diversity; a string of high-profile female musicians, from Taylor Swift to Dua Lipa, have exposed the sexism they've experienced; and in 2018, gender pay gap data from the three main music labels in the UK revealed that women were being paid almost 30% less than their male colleagues.

In recent years, there have been major triumphs for women in among the bleak reality, of course. Ariana Grande became the first woman to knock herself off the number one spot in the UK in 2019. Kylie not only had a ginormous crowd watching her play the Legends slot at Glastonbury, but 3.2 million viewers also tuned in from home – making it the most-watched moment in the festival's history. It's even sweeter that she was 51 at the time.

At the 2020 Oscars, Hildur Guðnadóttir became only the third female composer to win the Academy Award for Best Original Score, for her work on *Joker*. She's now one trophy away from having the coveted EGOT (that's an Emmy, Grammy, Oscar and Tony) that only four other women – Helen Hayes, Rita Moreno, Audrey Hepburn and Whoopi Goldberg – have ever won.

The women still fighting for equality in the 21st-century music industry follow in the tuneful wake of the formidable musical dames who came before them. Many are household names, and others have been all but erased from the history books: but every single one is a brilliant badass.

1. **What was the rallying cry of Riot Grrrl pioneer and Bikini Kill frontwoman Kathleen Hanna during her band's early days? (1)**

    a) Smash the patriarchy
    b) Girls to the front
    c) Rebel women unite

2. **Author and columnist Caitlin Moran started her journalistic career at the age of 16 on which music publication? (1)**

    a) *Melody Maker*
    b) *Classic FM Magazine*
    c) *Kerrang!*

3. **Match the frontwoman to their otherwise all-male band. (1 point for each correct answer)**

Debbie Harry	The Pretenders
Shirley Manson	The Cranberries
Chrissie Hynde	The Banshees
Karen O	Blondie
Gladys Knight	Yeah Yeah Yeahs
Gwen Stefani	Garbage
Dolores O'Riordan	The Pips
Siouxsie Sioux	No Doubt

4. **How did Kate Bush get her nickname Ee-ee? (1)**

   a) It was the sound she made while she was running up a hill
   b) It was the sound she made as she accepted her BRIT Award in 1987
   c) It was the sound she made before attacking her opponent during karate training

5. **Match these musicians to their real first names. (1 point for each correct answer)**

Joni Mitchell	Melissa
Lady Gaga	Anna Mae
Etta James	Roberta
Lizzo	Pauline
Kiki Dee	Jamesetta
Tina Turner	Yvette
Chaka Khan	Stefani

6. **Some of the catchiest TV theme tunes have been written and performed by women. Name the musicians behind these hummable numbers. (2 points for each correct answer)**

   a) *Gilmore Girls*
   b) *Orange is the New Black*

c) *Freaks and Geeks*
d) *New Girl*
e) *Doctor Who*

7. **Find these 15 classical composers in the wordsearch. (2)**

Amy Beach

Augusta Holmès

Barbara Strozzi

Clara Schumann

Ethel Smyth

Fanny Mendelssohn

Florence Price

Hildegard of Bingen

Lili Boulanger

Louise Farrenc

Marianna Martines

Min Huifen

Nadia Boulanger

Rebecca Clarke

Zenobia Powell Perry

H	T	Y	M	S	L	E	H	T	E	M	H	B	E	A	M	F	Y
S	B	W	Q	I	M	I	N	I	B	F	S	E	C	L	A	R	N
E	A	R	V	Y	N	T	O	U	I	A	C	A	I	D	R	E	N
M	R	E	I	E	C	H	S	C	N	N	H	D	R	E	I	B	A
L	B	G	P	C	N	I	U	L	G	N	U	I	P	S	A	E	M
O	A	N	Q	S	E	L	N	I	S	Y	L	L	E	O	N	C	U
H	R	A	G	A	R	O	G	L	F	M	L	W	C	N	N	C	H
A	A	L	B	X	R	U	A	I	C	E	Y	H	N	J	A	A	C
T	S	U	R	T	A	M	M	B	W	N	N	C	E	E	M	C	S
S	T	O	A	D	F	Z	Z	O	E	D	S	A	R	N	A	L	A
U	R	B	B	C	E	G	P	U	R	E	T	E	O	N	R	A	R
G	O	A	U	C	S	A	R	L	D	L	R	B	L	Y	T	R	A
U	Z	I	X	E	I	R	I	A	N	S	O	Y	F	N	I	K	L
A	Z	D	Z	B	U	D	C	N	A	S	Z	M	E	N	N	E	C
D	I	A	O	G	O	H	L	G	M	O	D	A	P	A	E	Z	T
W	F	N	D	E	L	S	S	E	C	H	C	T	Y	M	S	Z	Y
H	E	F	O	X	L	G	E	R	U	N	O	L	F	U	G	U	A
Z	N	E	G	N	I	B	F	O	D	R	A	G	E	D	L	I	H

8. True or false? No women have been nominated for more than 50 Grammys. (1)

_____

9. She dubbed the singing voices of Audrey Hepburn in *My Fair Lady*, Deborah Kerr in *The King and I* and Natalie Wood in *West Side Story*, as well as singing the high notes in 'Diamonds are a Girl's Best Friend' for Marilyn Monroe in *Gentlemen Prefer Blondes*. But can you name Hollywood's most famous ghost singer? (3)

_____

10. Name that tune! These opening lines were all performed by superstar women. Bonus points for correctly guessing what comes next. (1 point for naming the artist, an extra 1 point for each correct next line)

Lyric	Artist	Song Title	What Comes Next
Tumble outta bed and I stumble to the kitchen			
They paved paradise, and put up a parking lot			
Summertime, and the living is easy			
Birds flying high, you know how I feel			
Lucky you were born that far away so			
If you need me, call me			

11. **Who wrote these hits? (Hint: it wasn't the women who are most famous for singing them.) (2 points for each correct answer)**

'I Will Always Love You' by Whitney Houston

_____

'Party In The U.S.A.' by Miley Cyrus

_____

'Diamonds' by Rihanna

_____

'Breakaway' by Kelly Clarkson

_____

'Till The World Ends' by Britney Spears

_____

'(You Make Me Feel Like) A Natural Woman' by Aretha Franklin

_____

PHYSICAL EDUCATION

Whether you spent your schooldays forging notes from your mum in a desperate attempt to skip cross-country running, or impatiently counted down the minutes until it was time to get outside and kick a ball, it's difficult not to be impressed by the world's greatest sportswomen.

They're determined, dedicated and, let's face it, hard as nails. But on top of the gruelling training, the crack-of-dawn starts, the injuries and the defeats, they also have to deal with endless speculation about their clothes, their bodies and their love lives.

'Twas ever thus, of course. In the olden days, many (men) believed that women simply weren't built for sports – that they were too weak, or that their reproductive organs would become damaged, or that menstruation meant they couldn't possibly participate (periods have also been blamed for killing bees and making bacon go off).

None of that stopped women competing, however. In Ancient Greece, they were banned from taking part in the Olympics (married women couldn't even be spectators), but the Heraean Games were organised every four years by a committee of 16 women to take place alongside the male-only event. The only downside was that the eligible maidens who raced had to do so with their right breast flapping around for all to see, thanks to their traditional tunics, but at least a sporting revolution was afoot.

Fast-forward two millennia, and sport among women of the upper classes and aristocracy became popular. Mary, Queen of Scots was the first woman in Scotland to play golf, and she donned men's breeches for tennis matches. Archery, horse riding, cricket and croquet were all acceptable activities for delicate ladies, and the advent of the bicycle was a turning point in women's participation in – and enjoyment of – sports.

As the decades went on, more and more groundbreaking women proved that wombs were no obstacle to sporting glory, but the fight for equality isn't over yet. There's the ongoing issue of money, as the crowd chanting 'EQUAL PAY, EQUAL PAY!' at the final whistle of the Women's World Cup in 2019 reminded us. Still, the firsts are coming thick and fast, even now – the 2012 London Olympics were the first in which women competed in every single sport, and all participating countries had women on their teams.

So, lace up your trainers, limber up and get ready to give your brain muscles a workout with some of the most incredible sporting women, past and present.

1. Simone Biles was hospitalised with a kidney stone the night before the 2018 World Artistic Gymnastics Championships in Doha, Qatar. She went on to become the first American to win a medal in every event at a single world championship, including three individual golds. What did she affectionately name her pesky kidney stone? (1)

   a) The Doha Pearl
   b) Brandon K. Biles
   c) The Gold Growth

2. She's the fastest British woman in history, and has medals and trophies galore, but what very special honour did Dina Asher-Smith receive in 2020 to celebrate International Women's Day? (2)

   _____

3. Babe Didrikson Zaharias is best remembered as a champion golfer. What made her appearance at the 1932 Olympics particularly notable? (2)

   a) She was one of the equestrian commentators
   b) She competed with a broken ankle
   c) She won three track and field medals

4. **Mademoiselle De Lafontaine was the first professional ballerina. What did she do when she retired? (2)**

    a) Joined a convent
    b) Opened a bakery
    c) Became a motor racing star

5. **True or false? Fanny Blankers-Koen was 16 when she won four gold track and field medals at the 1948 London Olympics. (1)**

    _____

6. **When was the ban on women's football lifted in the UK? (2)**

Dick, Kerr Ladies F.C. in 1922.

_____

7. 'Our Lionesses go back to being mothers, partners and daughters today, but they have taken on another title – heroes.' Who managed to relegate the mighty women of England's football squad in one misjudged tweet? (1)

a) Former Prime Minister David Cameron
b) The Football Association
c) Prince William

'AT THE END OF THE DAY, IF I CAN SAY I HAD FUN, IT WAS A GOOD DAY.'

SIMONE BILES

8. These women all won their own battles of the sexes.
   Can you name them? (2 points for each correct answer)

a)

b)

c)

d)

e)

f)

9. Can you match these sporting women to their groundbreaking firsts? (2 points for each correct answer)

Gertrude Ederle	First woman to officially run the Boston Marathon
Hélène de Pourtalès	First woman to win the gruelling 268-mile Spine Race
Kathrine Switzer	First woman to win Olympic gold
Jasmin Paris	First woman to ride at a major British racecourse wearing a hijab
Khadijah Mellah	First American woman to win three gold medals at a single Olympic Games
Wilma Rudolph	First woman to swim the Channel

10. The Royal & Ancient Golf Club of St Andrews is the oldest, most prestigious golf club in the world. It was founded in 1754, but when were women permitted to join? (1)

a) 1850   b) 1987   c) 2014

11. **Unscramble these words to find four items of clothing that women have been prevented from wearing during sporting events. (1 point for each correct answer)**

ACT IT US _ _ _ _ _ _ _

HORSTS _ _ _ _ _ _

BARK NIP _ _ _ _ / _ _ _

AH JIB _ _ _ _ _

HISTORY

It should come as no surprise that the achievements of women throughout history are lesser-known: history was written by men.

But there were women making waves throughout history in myriad ways, on the throne and on the battle-field. The women in this chapter raised armies alongside raising children. They helped win wars as well as starting them. They made decisions that changed the course of the world.

Not every woman in this chapter is remembered for positive reasons, but nothing is achieved by erasing the grubbier elements of women's history. It's true that Coco Chanel was an incredible fashion designer; it's also possible she acted as a Nazi agent. Our childhood nostalgia for Enid Blyton's books doesn't wipe away her racism. One truth doesn't erase another. The more we learn about our history, the easier it is to determine what influences our modern world.

When we are taught about men throughout history, we learn about every facet of their lives: the good and the bad. A man is allowed to be a terrible person while still being celebrated for his achievements (Ernest Hemingway and Alfred Hitchcock both spring to mind). Women are not afforded such luxury. Women in history are good or bad. They are the saviour or the villain. Never both. And as a result, we're never quite given the whole picture.

This chapter covers the good, the bad, and sometimes the ugly parts of women through the ages. The course of history – particularly when it came to women – was messy and rough around the edges. It was, sometimes, bloody carnage. It was never smooth and perhaps we shouldn't want it to be. Perhaps we should be striving for truth, whatever light that paints us in.

1. **The Bletchley Park Estate in Buckinghamshire became the centre for cryptanalysis during WW2. How many women worked there? (1)**

   a) None   b) 8,000   c) 500

2. **Match the queen with the unusual death. (1 point for each correct answer)**

Empress Elisabeth of Austria	A stroke in the bathroom
Caroline of Ansbach	Forced imprisonment by her son
Lady Jane Grey	Strangulated bowel burst
Cleopatra	Drowned while her subjects watched
Sunanda Kumariratana	Death by suicide with a snake
Catherine the Great	Wounded in battle
Rani Lakshmi Bai	Stabbed in the heart
Amalasuintha, ruler of the Ostrogoths	Murdered in the bath
Joanna of Castile	Beheaded for high treason

3. The Forty Elephants was an all-women group that ran for almost 200 years. What did they do? (2)

   a) They were keen greyhound gamblers
   b) They were interested in gardening and topiary
   c) They were a gang of jewel thieves

4. Approximately how many women across Europe were executed for witchcraft? (1)

   a) 500   b) 5,500   c) 60,000

5. Complete this wordsearch of Henry VIII's wives. (2)

C	E	R	R	O	R	H	W	J	D	B	S	E	C	N	D	F
P	A	D	U	D	X	D	X	E	N	R	E	A	W	Y	I	T
C	V	T	G	O	H	U	C	G	A	I	T	X	K	E	E	H
A	O	F	H	P	M	R	S	N	V	H	B	K	H	L	D	G
T	U	I	J	E	O	Y	R	U	E	U	U	T	D	O	S	K
H	C	T	A	V	R	G	E	R	R	J	T	V	T	B	R	X
E	S	N	I	K	X	I	I	S	E	V	P	S	M	E	E	Y
R	D	D	E	Q	C	N	N	I	E	X	I	T	C	N	K	K
I	C	U	I	C	E	F	E	E	H	N	E	V	H	N	D	X
N	Y	H	M	P	F	J	D	Y	O	C	A	X	E	A	E	Y
E	W	Q	A	E	Y	G	L	A	S	F	L	J	V	D	F	G
H	O	R	N	I	M	F	R	U	V	N	A	D	T	E	B	B
O	R	B	E	H	E	A	D	E	D	O	C	R	K	T	E	H
W	V	S	Y	I	Z	Y	Q	M	D	P	P	E	A	Q	S	L
A	C	N	K	T	F	G	C	A	O	D	E	A	K	G	M	S
R	S	E	V	E	L	C	F	O	E	N	N	A	E	X	O	H
D	Q	N	P	F	B	P	K	S	V	T	Z	I	I	P	Y	N

6. **Unscramble these philosophers. (2 points for each correct answer)**

   DARN HENNA HAT _ _ _ _ _ _ / _ _ _ _ _ _

   PARIAH CHIP _ _ _ _ _ _ _ _ _ _

   WANNA DECAY ONLY _ _ _ _ / _ _ _ _ / _ _ _ _ _ _

   LOAF HIPPO PIT _ _ _ _ _ _ _ _ / _ _ _ _

   LLAMA TYRES _ _ _ _ / _ _ _ _ _ _

7. **Which of these statements about Queen Victoria is false? (1)**

   a) She began the trend of brides wearing white on their wedding day
   b) Several assassination attempts were made against her
   c) She was the first British monarch to fly in a plane

8. **Can you name these abolitionists and civil rights activists? (2 points for each correct answer)**

a)

b)

c)

d)

e)

f)

9. **What unusual ingredient did Mary, Queen of Scots wash her face with? (2)**

   a) Honey   b) Salt   c) White wine

10. **Irena Sendler smuggled more than 2,500 Jewish children out of the Warsaw ghetto during the Second World War. One of the youngest was five-month-old Elżbieta Ficowska. How was she transported to safety? (2)**

    a) In a toolbox
    b) In a potato sack
    c) In a coffin

11. **Which London railway station might Boudicca be buried beneath? (1)**

ANSWERS

LITERATURE

1: a) Virginia Woolf
In her seminal essay, *A Room of One's Own*.

2:
Zora Neale Hurston. Despite being much-celebrated as an author and playwright during her lifetime, the appallingly low royalties afforded to her as a woman of colour (her most significant royalty earnings from any of her books amounted to $943.75) meant that she died penniless in 1960 and was buried in an unmarked grave. However, Alice Walker, for whom Hurston had been a great inspiration, travelled to the spot in 1973 and laid her own headstone as a mark of respect. Hurston remains a key figure in the literary canon today.

3:
Anne Brontë: Acton Bell
Louisa May Alcott: A.M. Barnard
Mary Ann Evans: George Eliot
Charlotte Brontë: Currer Bell
Amantine Lucile Aurore Dupin: George Sand
Emily Brontë: Ellis Bell
Violet Paget: Vernon Lee

Karen Blixen: Isak Dinesen
Alice Bradley Sheldon: James Tiptree Jr.

4: b) She lost her virginity

It is said that Mary Shelley lost her virginity on her mother's grave. Proving she is the original and best Goth, Mary reputedly chose her mother Mary Wollstonecraft's final resting place to do the deed with future husband Percy Shelley. Her taste for the ghoulish never waned; after Percy's death, she kept his heart in her desk drawer for decades.

5: a) Barbara Cartland

Ever the romantic, Barbara Cartland collected over 1,000 wedding dresses. 'They had their happiness; however quick and fleeting. . .' she wrote. 'By this stage in the war, love was about the only thing left unrationed.' She still found time to publish 723 books in her lifetime. Another 160 were published posthumously.

6: c) 18

Here are all of the women who have won the Booker Prize:

Bernice Rubens – *The Elected Member*, 1970

Nadine Gordimer (joint winner) – *The Conservationist*, 1974

Ruth Prawer Jhabvala – *Heat and Dust*, 1975

Iris Murdoch – *The Sea, The Sea*, 1978

Penelope Fitzgerald – *Offshore*, 1979

Anita Brookner – *Hotel du Lac*, 1984

Keri Hulme – *The Bone People*, 1985

Penelope Lively – *Moon Tiger*, 1987

A.S. Byatt – *Possession*, 1990

Pat Barker – *The Ghost Road*, 1995

Arundhati Roy – *The God of Small Things*, 1997

Margaret Atwood – *The Blind Assassin*, 2000

Kiran Desai – *The Inheritance of Loss*, 2006

Anne Enright – *The Gathering*, 2007

Hilary Mantel – *Wolf Hall*, 2009

Hilary Mantel – *Bring Up the Bodies*, 2012

Eleanor Catton – *The Luminaries*, 2013

Anna Burns – *Milkman*, 2018

Margaret Atwood – *The Testaments*, 2019

Bernadine Evaristo – *Girl, Woman, Other*, 2019

7: Hilary Mantel for *Wolf Hall* (2009) and *Bring Up the Bodies* (2012), and Margaret Atwood for *The Blind Assassin* (2000) and *The Testaments* (2019). Atwood and previous winner Iris Murdoch have received the most nominations – six each.

8: True. She sent an angry letter to Georges Duplaix in Paris that ended, 'If you don't make good your word to me, I will be over to shoot you with a bow and arrow in August. Love, Margaret Wise Brown'. She didn't have to follow up on her promise.

9:

a) Zadie Smith: *White Teeth*, *On Beauty*, *NW*, *Swing Time*

b) Toni Morrison: *Song of Solomon*, *Beloved*, *Paradise*, *God Help the Child*

c) Jacqueline Wilson: *The Story of Tracy Beaker*, *The Illustrated Mum*, *Hetty Feather*, *The Suitcase Kid*

d) Jilly Cooper: *Riders*, *Rivals*, *Polo*, *The Man Who Made Husbands Jealous*

e) Amy Tan: *The Joy Luck Club*, *The Kitchen God's Wife*, *The Bonesetter's Daughter*, *The Valley of Amazement*

f) Chimamanda Ngozi Adichie: *Half of a Yellow Sun*, *Americanah*, *Purple Hibiscus*, *We Should All Be Feminists*

g) Sarah Waters: *Tipping the Velvet*, *The Little Stranger*, *Fingersmith*, *The Night Watch*

10: Jane Austen. In fact, her books are filled with Regency slang that she invented or popularised. For example, 'if I've told you once, I've told you 100 times,' 'brace yourself,' and 'dress a salad'. Words and phrases from *Emma* have appeared in more than 300 entries in the *Oxford English Dictionary*. Bonus fact: in her spare time, Austen liked brewing her own beer.

11: c) Whisky, Ferraris and gambling
Françoise Sagan was the enfant terrible of the French literary scene. She lived fast and loose, spending her book profits in the casinos of Monte Carlo, crashing expensive cars and – if the rumours are true – taking such vast quantities of drugs that her dog once overdosed by sniffing her handkerchief.

12:

First lines
The Bell Jar, Sylvia Plath
Jane Eyre, Charlotte Brontë
Rebecca, Daphne du Maurier
Paradise, Toni Morrison
Oryx and Crake, Margaret Atwood
Wide Sargasso Sea, Jean Rhys
Little Women, Louisa May Alcott
Black Beauty, Anna Sewell
Middlemarch, George Eliot
The Color Purple, Alice Walker

Last lines

Frankenstein, Mary Shelley

Bridget Jones's Diary, Helen Fielding

Emma, Jane Austen

Mrs Dalloway, Virginia Woolf

The Awakening, Kate Chopin

The Handmaid's Tale, Margaret Atwood

GEOGRAPHY

1: a) Nellie Bly

Let's talk a bit more about **Ms Nellie Bly**. Not only did she travel around the world, she was also a pioneer of investigative journalism. Early on in her career she feigned being mentally unwell to get herself committed so she could report on the conditions in mental health institutions. In 1887, she published a book about her findings, *Ten Days in a Mad-House*, which is still in print today as part of the anthology, *Around the World in 72 Days*.

Martha Gellhorn was leaps and bounds more interesting than her husband, Ernest Hemingway (all four of his wives were). She was one of the world's first female war reporters and travelled across Europe to cover D-Day, the Blitz and, in her eighties, the US invasion of Panama.

Harriet Chalmers Adams spent her life travelling the world and writing about it for *National Geographic* magazine. However, she wasn't allowed to join the National Geographic Society because she was a woman. In 1925, she became the first president of the Society of Women Geographers instead.

2: c) 0

Jeanne Baret almost certainly discovered the much loved (and frequently Instagrammed) bougainvillea. However, as the name suggests, the expedition's leader, Louis Bougainville, took the credit despite it being unlikely that he ever searched for specimens himself.

Baret had disguised herself as a man, binding her chest with bandages, to join the voyage with French naturalist Philibert Commerson. The couple managed to keep her identity a secret for over a year. It's unknown exactly how it was discovered she was a woman, but Baret was forced to go into seclusion. She and Commerson couldn't return to France on the ship and they were forced to dock at Mauritius. It wasn't until 1774, possibly 1775, that Baret returned to France.

3: b) 50

Helen Thayer was 50 when she completed the expedition, with only her dog Charlie for company.

4:

Isabelle Eberhardt

Jeanne Baret

Isobel Gunn

Calamity Jane

Dervla Murphy

Lady Hester Stanhope

F	J	A	H	O	M	P	V	E	E	F	H	C	R	B	V	E	D
J	M	I	T	C	H	D	J	W	D	Q	D	X	J	K	D	P	E
P	Q	K	O	A	G	M	A	C	A	N	Y	E	C	V	T	O	R
L	T	U	B	W	U	L	M	J	G	Z	A	A	A	Y	C	H	V
Z	R	H	C	L	E	E	E	N	R	N	J	J	Y	L	P	N	L
Z	I	Y	L	A	K	N	S	S	N	W	L	U	N	C	D	A	A
I	S	A	B	E	L	L	E	E	B	E	R	H	A	R	D	T	M
L	C	H	P	N	G	A	B	H	U	G	H	K	T	T	P	S	U
U	G	M	N	P	A	A	M	L	U	G	O	I	S	Y	H	R	R
K	F	J	G	V	R	I	V	I	G	O	D	E	I	G	O	E	P
E	K	W	E	E	B	F	T	T	T	Y	R	H	R	V	V	T	H
G	Q	N	T	C	M	R	B	S	D	Y	A	Z	T	Z	F	S	Y
N	N	U	G	L	E	B	O	S	I	R	J	E	V	A	D	E	U
T	H	T	N	H	E	J	V	B	R	R	C	A	Q	K	U	H	L
Z	O	O	H	E	N	O	J	Y	I	D	H	N	N	K	E	Y	Z
M	U	V	J	K	M	P	T	N	Q	N	D	C	M	E	A	D	E
S	M	Q	U	I	R	J	T	J	Q	U	D	E	T	A	A	A	H
V	J	N	O	M	W	X	G	Q	E	V	M	E	X	N	W	L	X

5: b) A nail file

Evelyn found herself trapped in a deadly spider's web. Nephila spiders are known for their particularly strong webs and Cheesman discovered that struggling to get free only made the bonds of the web tighter. She was stuck for an hour before she was able to free herself with a nail file found in the seam of her pocket.

6:

Lady Hester Stanhope: Camel

Amelia Earhart: Aeroplane

Ellen MacArthur: Yacht

Isabella Bird: Horse (where she refused to sit side saddle)

Mary Kingsley: Canoe

Eva Dickson: Racing car

Polly Letofsky: Foot

Lady Grace Drummond-Hay: Zeppelin

Van Buren Sisters: Motorcycle

Annie Londonderry: Bicycle

7: It's true! Gertrude Bell also included a fur coat and her evening dresses as must-have travel items. For fancy sand dune soirées, obviously.

8: Namira Salim was also the first Pakistani to reach both the North and South Poles.

9: b) 13 years and 11 months

Malavath Poorna from India was just shy of her fourteenth birthday when she first reached the summit of the world's highest mountain in 2014. At 14, most of us were reading *Shout* magazine and making friendship bracelets.

10:

MANY CREPES – Mary Spence

HARM PIRATE – Marie Tharp

PAPILLARY SHELLS – Phyllis Pearsall

ABRASIVE HARKING – Kira B Shingareva

EEL ONLY FRECKLE – Florence Kelley

HANDSAW HI TIT – Shanawdithit

11: a) Ann Bancroft

Not the actress who played Mrs Robinson in *The Graduate*, that was Anne Bancroft with an 'e'. Not content with being the first woman to reach the North Pole by foot in 1986 in a 56-day expedition, this brilliant Bancroft led a four-woman expedition to the South Pole on skis in 1992. In 2001, with fellow explorer Liv Arnesen, she became one of the first women to cross Antarctica.

12:

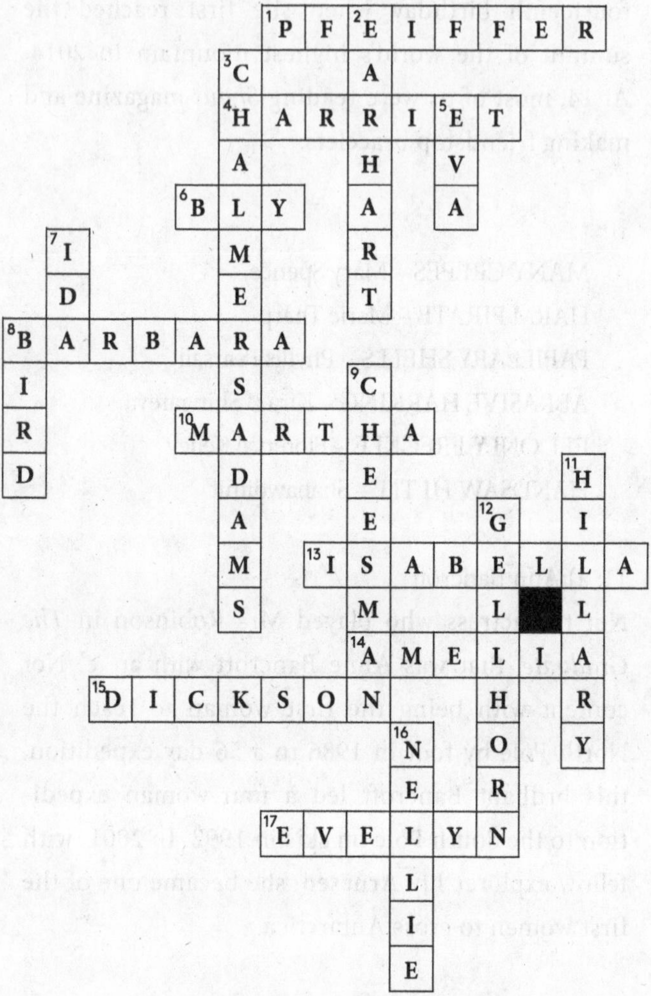
1 PFEIFFER
2 EARHART
3 CHALMERS ADAMS
4 HARRIET
5 EVA
6 BLY
7 ID
8 BARBARA
BIRD
9 CHEESMAN
10 MARTHA
11 HILLARY
12 GELLHORN
13 ISABELLA
14 AMELIA
15 DICKSON
16 NELLIE
17 EVELYN

MATHEMATICS

1: c) The second Tuesday in October

Ada Lovelace is often called the 'Enchantress of Numbers', and in fact she was one of the greatest mathematical minds in history. She was Lord Byron's daughter, his only legitimate child, and her mother pushed her to study maths and Science in the hope that she wouldn't inherit her father's erm . . . flamboyant and moody temperament.

Ada met inventor Charles Babbage in 1833 when she was just 17 – the pair were introduced to each other by her private tutor, Mary Somerville. They became friends and Ada worked on the language for Charles Babbage's mechanical computer, the Analytical Engine. The machine was created to handle complex calculations, but it was Lovelace who realised its potential to repeat patterns and build on the original number crunching. In her paper, she expanded on Babbage's work, and that of his assistants, suggesting that the machine could be used to create music and manipulate symbols. During her short life – Ada Lovelace died of cancer in 1852, aged just 36 – her work didn't attract the attention it deserved, but she's now thought to be the creator of the world's first computer programme.

2: c) She was denied her full degree

Like hundreds of other women, Joan Clarke's degree was in name only, so she never officially graduated with her double first in maths. Women weren't awarded full degrees from Cambridge until after the Second World War – the war that Clarke's work at Bletchley Park helped to shorten considerably.

3: a) Emmy Noether

In 1918, Emmy Noether's work revolutionised the field of physics. Her connection between conservation laws and symmetry laws helped physicists to understand the world's energy and solve several problems in the field. Noether's theorem might not be commonplace in our everyday chat, but 100 years on, it's still vital to the work of physicists. Where we rely on laws of physics to understand how our world works, Noether's theorem helps scientists understand those very laws.

4:

Margaret Hamilton	Project Apollo
Annie J. Easley	Cassini
Melba Roy	Project Echo
Barbara Paulson	The Viking Program
Dorothy Vaughan	SCOUT Launch Vehicle Program

Margaret Hamilton was the director of the Software Engineering Division at MIT's Instrumentation Laboratory. She was the lead developer on Apollo's flight software.

As well as working as a computer programmer specialising in FORTRAN and developing code for the Cassini launch to Saturn, **Annie J. Easley** went on to strive for equal opportunities within NASA.

Melba Roy's work tracked the Echo satellites. Her detailed computations led the way for orbital timetables, which allow millions of people to view the satellites as they pass overhead.

Barbara Paulson calculated trajectories by hand for much of her career. She was also a vital part in ensuring that the Viking Program to Mars was successful. Her time at NASA's Jet Propulsion Lab wasn't smooth sailing – when they found out she was pregnant in 1960, she was forced to quit.

As a 'human computer', **Dorothy Vaughan** was wary of actual computers taking over the women's jobs at NASA. So, she made herself indispensable and taught herself – and the women in her team – the computer programme FORTRAN. She became an expert in her field.

5: a) Mary Somerville

Scottish mathematician and science writer **Mary Somerville** was the first woman to be allowed into the Royal Astronomical Society. Her interest in science began when she was 15 and spotted some algebraic equations decorating the page of a fashion magazine. She set about learning how to solve them. Her studies in maths led to her career as a gifted science writer. In one of her books she wrote about a hypothetical planet perturbing Uranus – there was a 'wobble' in its orbit. Her theory led John Couch Adams to the discovery of Neptune in 1846.

Mathematician **Flora Philip** was one of the first women to graduate from Edinburgh University. **Sheila Scott Macintyre** was an accomplished Scottish mathematician. Both were members of the Edinburgh Mathematical Society.

6:

d) 1850

b) 1909

e) 1958

a) 2017

c) 2019

7: a) The Eiffel Tower

There are 72 names engraved around the sides of the Eiffel Tower, each recognising the scientists, engineers and mathematicians whose work and research helped create the tower. While Sophie Germain's theory of elasticity was used to create the famous tower, her name is not among them. In fact, no women are named.

8: a) She devoted her life to helping the poor

Although Maria Gaetana Agnesi was a hugely gifted mathematician, she didn't necessarily want it to be her career. Her father had always pushed her to pursue her studies but when he died, she turned her attention to her true calling – studying theology and helping those less fortunate. When she left the field of mathematics, she founded a shelter for the elderly.

9: c) Florence Nightingale

The Lady with the Lamp was one of the most important statisticians in history. Having decided to become a nurse, **Florence Nightingale** refused to marry and defied her parents to visit hospitals in Paris, London and Rome, before heading to Crimea. Here, she collected huge amounts of data on patients and the dire state of the hospitals and inadequate medical records. Her data showed that 16,000 of the 18,000 deaths weren't from war injuries but from preventable diseases. The changes she put in place made the hospitals more efficient and more sanitary, and she saved countless lives. The data she collected had a huge impact in reforming our healthcare system.

Clara Barton and **Edith Cavell** were also incredibly accomplished nurses. In 1881, Barton founded the American Red Cross and led the organisation for 23 years. British nurse Edith Cavell is celebrated for saving the lives of hundreds of troops from both sides during the First World War, saying, 'I can't stop while there are lives to be saved'. She was executed by a German firing squad in 1915 after her work was discovered.

10:

 a) 415

 b) 20

 c) 2,040

 d) 11,000

DRAMA

1: *The Hurt Locker*, awarded to Kathryn Bigelow in 2010.

Nomadland, awarded to Chloé Zhao in 2020.

The Power of the Dog, awarded to Jane Campion in 2021.

2: b) Wireless technology

Hedy Lamarr used bouncing radio frequencies – much like playing notes on a piano – to create an untraceable radio communications system. Her patent was awarded in 1942. However, Lamarr's invention wasn't the only one of its kind. Similar technology was being invented in Germany. Nikola Tesla also held a US patent – granted in 1903 – for technology that used two different radio frequencies, rather than one that bounced. While it's not quite the same, it's certainly in a very similar ballpark. Inventions often sprang from one idea to another, with inventors experimenting with existing forms to create something new to fit a need. Ideas are built on and evolve.

Whether she was first, last or somewhere in the middle, Hedy Lamarr's invention was still well before its time – it was another 20 years before her technology was used by the US military during the Cuban Missile Crisis, by which time her patent had expired and she never received a penny.

Lamarr's invention evolved again and similar technology was used in contemporary wireless devices. However, the bandwidth in her technology soon proved to be insufficient so it was quickly abandoned. Modern needs made way for further technology advancement.

3: b) 1660

It is believed that Margaret Hughes was the first female stage actress, playing the role of Desdemona in Shakespeare's *Othello* on 8 December 1660.

4:

RAYS DIDO – Doris Day

JEDI FOOTERS – Jodie Foster

UNHARDY BURPEE – Audrey Hepburn

VEILING HIVE – Vivien Leigh

NETTABLE CATCH – Cate Blanchett

HINTED PIPER – Tippi Hedren

RELAX COVEN – Laverne Cox

GOPHERWOOD GLIB – Whoopi Goldberg

AIRWORTHY HAT – Rita Hayworth

CHERRIED AILMENT – Marlene Dietrich

LAW COBRA – Clara Bow

BRAT AHEAD – Theda Bara

BRING DREAMING – Ingrid Bergman

LACUNA BALLER – Lauren Bacall

5: Just one – *Whatever Happened to Baby Jane?*

Although the feud between Bette Davis and Joan Crawford was thought to have been created by their film studios for publicity purposes, it went on to be very real. It's rumoured that Joan Crawford influenced the

Academy's decision for the Best Actress category and the gong went to Anne Bancroft for *The Miracle Worker*. Bancroft was performing on Broadway and unable to accept her award, but Crawford had graciously offered to accept it on her behalf and waltzed on stage, further taking the limelight away from her nominated co-star. *Whatever Happened to Baby Jane?* was Bette's last Oscar nomination.

6: a) Olivia de Havilland

In 1943, Olivia de Havilland fought Warner Bros. when the studio tried to force her to extend her contract, adding time she had been suspended from the studio to her end date. Bette Davis had attempted the same with her studio six years earlier and was unsuccessful, but the case almost ruined de Havilland's career. Warner Bros. blacklisted the actress and she didn't get a major role for two years. She came back swinging and won her first Oscar in 1947 for *To Each His Own*. Another followed in 1950 for *The Heiress*. Olivia de Havilland passed away in 2020, aged 104. De Havilland Law is still cited in the industry today.

7:

First black actress to win an Oscar	Hattie McDaniel
First Chinese star in Hollywood	Anna May Wong

First female director of Indian cinema	Fatma Begum
First black female film star	Josephine Baker
First named silent movie actress	Florence Lawrence
First Best Actress Oscar winner	Janet Gaynor
First female Hollywood stunt woman	Helen Gibson
First Indian talkie actress	Zubeida Begum Dhanrajgir

8:

a) ___ Wedding – *Monsoon Wedding*, Mira Nair

b) ___ Bird – *Lady Bird*, Greta Gerwig

c) The ___ Fairy – *The Cabbage Fairy*, Alice Guy-Blaché

d) Something's Gotta ___ – *Something's Gotta Give*, Nancy Meyers

e) The Trouble with ___ – *The Trouble with Angels*, Ida Lupino

f) ___ Face – *Saving Face*, Alice Wu

g) Fast Times at ___ High – *Fast Times at Ridgemont High*, Amy Heckerling

h) Bend it Like ___ – *Bend it Like Beckham*, Gurinder Chadha

i) Little ___ – *Little Women*, Gillian Armstrong (1994) Greta Gerwig (2019)

j) A ___ of Their Own – *A League of Their Own*, Penny Marshall

k) The ___ Suicides – *The Virgin Suicides*, Sofia Coppola

l) ___ Strength – *Double Strength*, Barbara Hammer

m) Zero ___ Thirty – *Zero Dark Thirty*, Kathryn Bigelow

n) A ___ in Time – *A Wrinkle in Time*, Ava DuVernay

o) You've Got ___ – *You've Got Mail*, Nora Ephron

p) ___ Strong – *Christopher Strong*, Dorothy Arzner

9: c) A lion called Neil

Neil occasionally slept in the same bed as Tippi Hedren's daughter Melanie Griffith (yes, that one), who needed facial reconstruction surgery after he mauled her on the set of the film *Roar*. Tippi has since said that letting a wild lion roam free was 'stupid beyond belief'. She's not wrong.

10:

a) Grace Kelly, *Rear Window*

b) Tippi Hedren, *The Birds*

c) Dorothy Lamour, *The Hurricane*

d) Audrey Hepburn, *Roman Holiday*

e) Hedy Lamarr, *Samson & Delilah*

f) Ingrid Bergman, *Notorious*

SCIENCE

1: a) They were all astronomers

Edward Pickering was the lead astronomer at Harvard in 1881 and hired women to work as 'Harvard Computers' because they were much cheaper to employ than men. However, obviously – being women – they weren't allowed to use complicated technology such as telescopes. They did all of their groundbreaking work manually.

2:

Discovered the Horsehead Nebula: Williamina Fleming

Classified over 350,000 stars: Annie Jump Cannon

Determined the sun's chemical composition: Cecilia Payne-Gaposchkin

Calculated the distances of stars from Earth: Henrietta Swan Leavitt

3: a) Marie Curie

Marie Curie was awarded the Nobel Prize for Physics in 1903 for her groundbreaking research in radiation, and then in 1911 she won the prize in Chemistry. She's one of only two people to have ever been awarded in two different categories. Her daughter, Irene Curie, went on to win a Nobel Prize in Chemistry in 1935 for her discovery of artificial radioactivity.

The first woman astronomer to publish a star catalogue: Antonia Maury

Williamina Fleming had actually been Edward Pickering's maid before she became part of his science team. She was only hired to prove a point to his male assistants about how easy classification work was.

Not only did **Annie Jump Cannon** manually classify over 350,000 stars, the system she created is still used today.

Cecilia Payne-Gaposchkin's discovery that the sun was mainly made up of hydrogen and helium was discredited by Pickering.

Henrietta Swan Leavitt's discovery was complex but crucial to our understanding of space – she worked out that some stars had a different level of brightness that could be quantified and used as a way of measuring distance. She essentially mapped the universe. Without her work – all done manually – Hubble may not have been able to measure distances between the stars. Of course, Hubble never credited her discovery.

Antonia Maury worked on Jump Cannon's classification system, but she was particularly interested in the luminosity of the stars and built a system around this area. Of course, this was also discredited by Pickering until it was confirmed by another male astronomer – Ejnar Hertzsprung. Maury's star catalogue was the first published under a woman's name.

4: b) Nuclear fission

Lise Meitner was part of the team of scientists that discovered nuclear fission. She had discovered several isotopes while working with Otto Hahn, and the pair went on to work together until she left Germany when Hitler came to power. Hahn stayed in Berlin but called upon Meitner to help decipher the results of his work – she theorised that he had split a uranium atom to create the new element barium, and it's thought that her nephew, Otto Frisch, coined the term 'fission' (although the idea of nuclear fission itself was first discussed by another female scientist – German chemist Ida Noddack). Hahn published his paper without mentioning the input of his fellow scientists and won the Nobel Prize in 1944.

Meitner was notably omitted from receiving a Nobel Prize for any of her work. She was nominated no less than 48 times throughout her career.

Upon returning to science after working as a nurse during the Second World War, Meitner discovered a physical phenomenon in atoms. It's now known as the Auger effect – named after the French chemist Pierre Victor Auger, who made the discovery independently a year later. British physicist James Chadwick discovered the neutron in 1932 but he acknowledged that Meitner would have been the first to make the discovery had she been given the resources and support to do so.

5: c) 1992

Before becoming an astronaut, Mae Jemison was actually a doctor for the Peace Corps in Sierra Leone and Liberia. On 12 September 1992, Jemison made her first flight into space aboard the *Endeavour*.

6:

    a) Rhenium, Ida Noddack

    b) Polonium, Marie Curie

    c) Radium, also Marie Curie

    d) Kevlar, Stephanie Kwolek

    e) DNA Structure, Rosalind Franklin

    f) BRCA Gene, Mary-Claire King

    g) Dark Matter, Vera Rubin

    h) Radio Pulsars, Jocelyn Bell Burnell

    i) Nuclear Shell, Maria Goeppert Mayer

7:

The 25 women awarded a Nobel Prize in science are:

Donna Strickland

Maria Goeppert Mayer

Marie Curie

Frances H. Arnold
Ada E. Yonath
Dorothy Crowfoot Hodgkin
Irène Joliot-Curie
Tu Youyou
May-Britt Moser
Elizabeth H. Blackburn
Carol W. Greider
Françoise Barré-Sinoussi
Linda B. Buck
Christiane Nüsslein-Volhard
Gertrude B. Elion
Rita Levi-Montalcini
Barbara McClintock
Rosalyn Yalow
Gerty Cori
Anne L'Huillier
Katalin Karikó
Carolyn Bertozzi
Andrea M. Ghez
Emmanuelle Charpentier
Jennifer A. Doudna

8: a) The first group of women to study medicine at university

The Edinburgh Seven were the first group of women to study medicine at a British university. Sophia Jex-Blake applied to study medicine at Edinburgh University in 1869, but the university court rejected her application, stating that they couldn't accommodate the needs of 'one lady'. She ran an advert to find more women to join her, and one lady became seven. Their cause had wide support across the science community – even Charles Darwin was behind them – and their fight paved the way for women to study medicine. Sadly, there wasn't a secret group of Victorian science-loving detective writers.

The Edinburgh Seven were:

Sophia Jex-Blake
Isabel Thorne
Edith Pechey
Matilda Chaplin
Helen Evans
Mary Anderson
Emily Bovell

9: b) Butterfly
It was actually silkworms that caught Maria Sibylla Merian's attention as a teenager. She became fascinated with the process of metamorphosis in insects, particularly caterpillars. She took an unusual approach in her illustrations and painted the subject of her studies in their full life cycle, and in connection with their ecological surroundings.

In 1705 she published *Metamorphosis insectorum Surinamensium*, but it was not until 2018 that a rare butterfly from Panama was named *Catasticta sibyllae* in her honour.

10: a) The tongue twister 'She Sells Seashells on the Seashore'

The tongue twister is said to refer to Mary Anning, who lived on the Dorset coastline and was often found scouring the beach for fossils. Anning's discoveries were regularly claimed by scientists to be fake, despite the fact that they bought her fossils for their own research, and they rarely credited her in their papers.

POLITICS

1. American. Virginia-born Nancy Astor became MP for Plymouth Sutton in 1919. She wasn't actually the first woman to be elected to Westminster, however – Irish politician Constance Markievicz won for Sinn Féin in 1918 but didn't take up her seat in accordance with her party's policies. On her first day in Parliament, Nancy was reprimanded for chatting. Winston Churchill once told her, 'I find a woman's intrusion into the House of Commons as embarrassing as if she burst into my bathroom

when I had nothing to defend myself, not even a sponge.' Her reply? 'You are not handsome enough to have worries of that kind.'

2. False. The Hampton Court Harridan, as she was known to her enemies, was an Indian princess and Queen Victoria's beloved goddaughter. Her royal connections made her political beliefs – namely, that women should have the right to vote – all the more shocking to the establishment.

3:

Love trumps hate: Hillary Clinton

Unbought and unbossed: Shirley Chisholm

¡No pasarán!: Pussy Riot

When they go low, we go high: Michelle Obama

Let's do this: Jacinda Ardern

Women are equal to everything: Lady Hale

Deeds, not words: Emmeline Pankhurst

Hillary Clinton had a lot of slogans during her 2016 presidential campaign, including the succinct-but-effective 'Love trumps hate'.

Shirley Chisholm was the first black major-party presidential candidate. Her unforgettable campaign slogan was 'Unbought and unbossed'.

It's no surprise Russian feminist protest punk band **Pussy Riot** are such fans of the rallying cry '¡No pasarán!' The Spanish translation of 'They shall not pass' was made famous by Republican fighter Dolores Ibárruri during the Spanish Civil War and has been used as a slogan across the globe since the First World War. Members of the band were jailed for hooliganism in 2012, following an anti-Putin performance.

As soon as **Michelle Obama** said, 'When they go low, we go high' in a speech supporting Hillary Clinton at the 2016 Democratic National Convention, it was obvious it was going to become one of the motivational quotes of the century.

New Zealand's **Jacinda Ardern** opted for a simple 'Let's do this' as her party's slogan during the 2017 General Election. She did indeed do it.

Lady Hale, the first female President of the Supreme Court and undisputed Queen of Spider Brooches, chose *Omnia feminae aequissimae* as her official motto. The Latin translates into English as 'Women are equal to everything'.

'Deeds, not words' became the motto of the Women's Social and Political Union, founded by **Emmeline Pankhurst** in 1903. It later became synonymous with the wider suffragette cause.

4: c) Bread shortages

More than 7,000 angry women marched 12 miles from the markets of Paris to the Palace of Versailles to confront Louis XVI about the scarcity and high price of bread. People were hungry, and the women wanted the king to move to the city and see what life was really like for Parisians. Upon hearing their plight, Marie Antoinette is rumoured to have uttered, '*Qu'ils mangent de la brioche*' ('Let them eat cake'), although there's no record of her actually saying it.

5:

COURTESAN LINGO – Nicola Sturgeon

A GLEAM KERNEL – Angela Merkel

A DRAIN HIDING – Indira Gandhi

ABOARD KNIT SKIRT JOT – Katrín Jakobsdóttir

TEETERED KNIFE MRS – Mette Frederiksen

AREA THYMES – Theresa May

6: a) Rwanda

In Rwanda, at the 2018 election, 61% of seats were won by women. Cuba and Bolivia are also doing pretty well, though – they take the second- and third-place spots, both with 53% of their parliamentary seats filled by women. In 39th position is the UK, with women winning 34% of seats in the House of Commons at the

2019 General Election. The US is lagging far behind at number 75 – women make up less than a quarter of the House of Representatives.

7: Alexandria Ocasio-Cortez. She's the youngest woman ever to serve in the United States Congress, and she got there with a grassroots, people-funded campaign.

8:

Q	D	Y	X	I	T	T	U	M	L	L	U	J	L	B	W	E	F
M	E	N	S	R	E	S	P	O	N	S	I	B	I	L	I	T	Y
E	V	N	O	I	T	I	U	T	N	I	E	L	A	M	E	F	L
T	L	E	O	P	C	A	E	S	D	N	O	R	P	Q	V	U	D
A	O	E	N	R	E	N	B	I	S	G	T	S	Z	O	H	E	C
R	G	A	C	K	M	R	U	E	Y	V	B	U	F	D	Y	I	L
H	J	T	O	O	C	O	N	T	R	O	L	L	I	N	G	L	E
T	U	S	W	H	E	F	U	T	A	H	V	F	P	O	N	A	S
R	Z	A	P	G	G	E	R	S	C	K	U	J	L	I	X	U	S
I	T	R	H	A	M	G	Y	W	H	E	I	Y	B	T	Q	R	U
B	M	J	O	B	Q	M	F	K	M	A	L	E	V	U	T	A	H
G	D	A	I	Y	E	E	S	A	E	D	T	L	I	N	G	C	Z
N	W	I	F	X	R	N	K	C	A	H	R	S	G	W	O	I	Q
I	T	N	E	M	I	T	N	E	S	F	O	S	T	S	U	G	C
L	N	G	V	A	Y	I	D	J	L	P	S	G	K	X	S	U	I
L	E	S	P	L	A	C	K	O	F	J	U	D	G	M	E	N	T
A	Y	E	B	D	R	E	T	P	G	K	P	C	T	O	N	C	S
F	E	M	A	P	S	A	R	W	U	X	I	O	H	L	D	G	J

Deadly logic

Arthur Beck, MP for Saffron Walden, was clearly a master in backhanded compliments. 'I daresay that the idealism of the feminine mind and its deadly logic which we have all experienced in private life are qualities superior to those of men,' he said, before ruining it with: 'but I do say that in governing a great country and in considering the problems which we have to consider every day in this House such qualities are not valuable, but destructive.'

Female intuition

Godfrey Collins, MP for Greenock, took a similar approach: 'Intuition is far more largely developed in women than in men, but instinct and intuition, although good guides, are not the best masters so far as Parliament is concerned.'

Enormous hats

Rowland Hunt, MP for Ludlow, was extremely concerned about millinery. 'There are obvious disadvantages about having women in Parliament. I do not know what is going to be done about their hats. Are they going to wear hats or not going to wear hats? If you ordered them not to wear hats, you might be absolutely certain that they would insist on wearing them. How is a poor little man to get on with a couple of women wearing enormous hats in front of him?' Hunt was also worried about the possibility of a female Speaker:

'We might have to address the Chair as "Mrs Speaker, Ma'am," for all we could tell.' The horror!

Gusts of sentiment
Frederick Banbury, MP for City of London, thought women were simply too temperamental to cope with the important business of voting. 'Women are likely to be affected by gusts and waves of sentiment,' he explained.

Too controlling
'We are controlled and worried enough by women,' said Sir James Grant, MP for Whitehaven. Poor James.

Men's responsibility
Sir Charles Henry, MP for Wellington, tried a different tack. He claimed that 'One of the greatest features in connection with this country is the responsibility of men towards women.' Yeah, nice try.

Falling birth rate
According to Sir Charles Hobhouse, MP for Bristol East, giving women the vote would 'mean an immense destruction of the population of the country'. Hobhouse was clearly prone to catastrophising.

ANSWERS

Lack of judgment
John Henderson, MP for Aberdeenshire West, simply couldn't believe that a woman described the Prime Minister as 'an old fossil', and he used this as evidence that people 'who exhibit such a want of judgment, and such a lack of perception of actual facts' should never be allowed to vote.

9:
a) The Dagenham machinists were famous for the 1968 strike at the Ford factory, where they were being paid far less than their male colleagues. Their protests led to the Equal Pay Act being passed in 1970, although it took a second strike in 1984 for them to actually get paid the same as the men.

b) Jayaben Desai led workers at the Grunwick film-processing lab in northwest London in a strike in 1976 against poor working conditions. Mrs Desai, as she always preferred to be known, did much to improve the lives of immigrant workers.

c) The Matchgirls' Strike of 1888 saw the women and girls working at the Bryant & May match factory in London protest against the terrible conditions and serious health risks – in particular 'phossy jaw', the nickname for the horrific necrosis caused by working with white phosphorus, which led to rotting jawbones that glowed in the dark. Aided by activist Annie Besant, their terms were met, and in 1901, Bryant & May stopped using the toxic substance.

d) The International Ladies' Garment Workers' Union was one of the biggest trade unions in America, with a predominantly female membership. Their most memorable industrial action was the New York Shirtwaist Strike of 1909, when 20,000 mainly Jewish women, led by Clara Lemlich, took to the streets to demand higher wages.

e) When the mostly female workforce of the Timex factory in Dundee went on strike in 1993, they made history – it was one of the most savage picket lines since the UK miners' strike. The women there, who had made our ZX Spectrum computers throughout the '80s, were protesting mass layoffs. Sadly, their seven-month strike ended with the closure of the factory.

10: b) Appoint someone to cover her maternity leave
Stella Creasy recruited a locum MP to look after her Walthamstow constituents for seven months when she

had daughter Hettie. She is a staunch campaigner for better maternity rights for MPs.

11: In short, suffragists were peaceful, and suffragettes were militant. Millicent Fawcett, founder of the National Union of Women's Suffrage Societies, was a suffragist; Emmeline Pankhurst, founder of the Women's Social and Political Union, was a suffragette. They had different views but a common goal, and their combined efforts won women the vote.

ART AND DESIGN

1:
- a) *Glamour*
- b) *Seventeen*
- c) *Mademoiselle*
- d) *Charm*
- e) *Vogue*
- f) *Vanity Fair*

2: a) An omelette made from their own hair
Leonora Carrington crept into her guests' bedrooms at night and snipped strands of their hair, before cooking it up in an omelette for breakfast the following morning. Her culinary inventiveness didn't stop there: she was particularly fond of elaborate 16th-century banquets and

once served the French writer and poet André Breton a hare stuffed with oysters.

3:

a) Vivienne Westwood made her first pair of pirate boots in 1981, and the style is still sold today.

b) Diane von Furstenberg is the undisputed queen of the wrap dress – hers are flattering, comfortable and failsafe. Many believe she invented the style, but 'hooverettes' were early examples of wrap dresses – albeit ones specifically designed to do the housework in.

c) Katharine Hamnett launched her oversized political slogan T-shirts in 1981. She's also renowned in the industry for her ethical business principles.

d) Mary Quant shook up the British high street in the Swinging Sixties with miniskirts, hot pants and bold tights.

e) Rei Kawakubo founded Comme des Garçons in 1969. The label is known for its bold, unique shapes and avant-garde designs.

f) Vera Wang is world-famous for her gorgeous wedding dresses. She also designs costumes for figure skaters (she's a talented skater who tried out for the US Olympic ice-skating team in 1968) and was one of *Vogue*'s youngest-ever fashion editors.

4:

    WAND JEER – Jane Drew
    BARONIAL BID – Lina Bo Bardi
    A HARMONY MIFFING IRON – Marion Mahony Griffin
    A BEELINE REVENGE LORRY – Beverly Loraine Greene
    MANORIAL JUG – Julia Morgan

Jane Drew was an English Modernist architect and town planner who began work at a time when there were very few women in architecture. Her first practice was all-female.

Lina Bo Bardi was a pioneering Brazilian architect with a focus on creating buildings for everyday people – as opposed to the rich and famous – to use and enjoy.

Marion Mahony Griffin was one of the world's first licensed female architects. She was a key figure in the Prairie School, which was characterised by buildings that are designed to integrate with the landscape and have an emphasis on horizontal lines.

Beverly Loraine Greene became a licensed architect in 1942 – she was the first African-American woman to do so.

Julia Morgan designed more than 700 of California's most notable buildings during her career. As well as looking lovely, they also made use of materials that could survive earthquakes.

5: c) Monopoly

Elizabeth Magie's version of The Landlord's Game had a lot of the similar elements that we all know and love from Monopoly (although fondness for the game really depends on who gets to be the Scottie dog). Parker had previously published Magie's games, and despite buying the rights to The Landlord's Game for $500, they never gave her credit for the role it played in the creation of Monopoly.

There have been dozens of iterations of the property trading board game since it first launched, from those styled on New York to *The Lord of the Rings*. In 2019, Parker released a Ms Monopoly game which switched things up so women made more money than men and rather than properties, inventions by women were featured around the board. Ms Magie wasn't included.

6: a) In her car

Georgia O'Keeffe had her Ford Model A customised so she could remove the driver's seat, swivel the passenger seat, and then place her paintings on the back seat to work on them. Why? She lived in New Mexico, and her clever mobile studio provided shade from the desert sun, as well as keeping out pesky bees.

7:

a) Orla Kiely is best known for her stem prints. She started out designing hats, but swapped to handbags when her father commented that all the women at London Fashion Week were carrying bags, but none were wearing hats.

b) Lucienne Day was one of the leading textile designers of the 1950s and '60s. *Calyx* is her most famous design, created for the Festival of Britain.

c) Anni Albers was one of the leading lights of the Bauhaus, whose work blurred the lines between craft and art.

d) Astrid Sampe was a pioneering Swedish textile designer, combining modern methods with elements of traditional Nordic design.

8: It's true! In 1953, bedbound due to her rapidly declining health (childhood polio and possible spina bifida caused her a lifetime of chronic pain and resulted in over 30 surgeries – including having her leg amputated), Frida Kahlo was loath to miss her big night, so she rocked up in an ambulance and was carried into the gallery on a stretcher. She spent the evening chatting to guests from the comfort of a four-poster bed adorned with papier-mâché skeletons.

9: b) Sculpture

Edmonia Lewis's beautiful marble sculptures had a distinctly neoclassical style, but their themes related to black and indigenous people. She cleverly and subtly turned tradition on its head and shook up the 19th-century art world.

10:

AXMAN CHIEF – Fax machine

TWIN GLACIAL – Call waiting

HOPE TO LUNCHEONETTE – Touch-tone telephone

SPIFLICATE COBBER – Fibre-optic cables

ACE DRILL – Caller ID

11:

Carmela Vitale	Pizza saver
Agnes Marshall	Ice cream maker
Melitta Bentz	Paper coffee filters
Florence Parpart	Electric refrigerator
Ruth Graves Wakefield	Chocolate chip cookie

Carmela Vitale's 'pizza saver' is that little plastic table that sits in the middle of your pizza. It stops the box from sinking so you don't find half of your toppings stuck to the lid when you get the delivery. While

Carmela held the patent from 1985, it's unlikely she ever made any money from her invention.

Dubbed 'Queen of Ices', **Agnes Marshall** was a popular Victorian cookery writer who wrote two books on 'fancy ices'. Her recipe books helped her make a significant income from selling dessert moulds and a hand-crank ice cream maker which froze the dessert while churning it – just like today's machines.

You'd be forgiven for thinking that coffee filters originated in Italy, but it was German entrepreneur **Melitta Bentz** who invented them after getting fed up with burnt coffee grounds and the mess from linen bag filters. Her first attempt at a new filter was with blotting paper from her son's school book. When her patent was awarded in 1908, she put her name on the company. Today, the Melitta coffee company employs over 5,000 people.

Florence Parpart didn't invent the first refrigerator – people had been using ice boxes for many years. However, in 1914 she invented the first fridge to run on electricity, which did away with the need to rely on a daily ice delivery.

Can you be the sole inventor of a recipe? **Ruth Graves Wakefield** would say so. Her chocolate chip cookies, or Toll House Cookies as they're better known, were a huge hit at her inn in Massachusetts. When she published the recipe in 1938, it was so popular that Nestlé's semi-sweet chocolate sales spiked and they bought the recipe from her. She struck an unusual business deal: one dollar and a lifetime supply of Nestlé chocolate.

MUSIC

1: b) Girls to the front
Kathleen Hanna and her bandmates made sure their female fans had a safe space and the best view at gigs, so they demanded that the men make way for the women so the girls could get to the front.

Bonus Kathleen fact: she came up with the name for Nirvana's most famous song, when she wrote 'Kurt smells like Teen Spirit' on his wall using a Sharpie. She had spotted a can of Teen Spirit deodorant in the supermarket earlier that day. Kurt had no idea it was a deodorant until months after the single was released.

2: a) *Melody Maker*
At an age when most of us thought the occasional evening babysitting or a Saturday afternoon spent sweeping up hair in the local salon was akin to hard labour, Caitlin Moran was embarking on her new job as a critic for beloved weekly music paper, *Melody Maker*. If that

doesn't sound precocious enough, she'd already written her first novel, *The Chronicles of Narmo*, the year before.

3:

Debbie Harry	Blondie
Shirley Manson	Garbage
Chrissie Hynde	The Pretenders
Karen O	Yeah Yeah Yeahs
Gladys Knight	The Pips
Gwen Stefani	No Doubt
Dolores O'Riordan	The Cranberries
Siouxsie Sioux	The Banshees

4: c) It was the sound she made before attacking her opponent during karate training

Kate's kiai – the short, sharp noise made during an attack in karate – was delightfully squeaky.

5:

Joni Mitchell	Roberta
Lady Gaga	Stefani
Etta James	Jamesetta
Lizzo	Melissa
Kiki Dee	Pauline
Tina Turner	Anna Mae
Chaka Khan	Yvette

6:

    a) *Gilmore Girls*: Carole King

    b) *Orange is the New Black*: Regina Spektor

    c) *Freaks and Geeks*: Joan Jett

    d) *New Girl*: Zooey Deschanel

    e) *Doctor Who*: Delia Derbyshire

Carole King composed 'Where You Lead' with lyricist Toni Stern. The two tweaked the lyrics to be less romantic and focus more on a mother-daughter relationship when *Gilmore Girls'* creator Amy Sherman-Palladino asked to use the song for her show. King re-recorded the new version with her own daughter, Louise Goffin, and she also made several guest appearances as the owner of the music shop in Stars Hollow.

Orange is the New Black creator Jenji Kohan listened to **Regina Spektor**'s back catalogue constantly while writing the show. It made sense, then, to ask her to compose and perform the theme song, too.

'Bad Reputation' was one of **Joan Jett**'s first solo singles. Her debut album after leaving The Runaways was rejected by 23 labels. She just went right ahead and started her own and released it herself.

As well as being an actor, *New Girl*'s **Zooey Deschanel** is one half of indie pop duo She & Him.

They even notched up a Grammy nomination for their song 'So Long' on the *Winnie the Pooh* soundtrack.

Delia Derbyshire arranged *Doctor Who*'s iconic theme song in 1963 and is now regarded as a pioneer of electronic music. She didn't get an official credit for creating the music until 2013 – 12 years after her death.

7:

H	T	Y	M	S	L	E	H	T	E	M	H	B	E	A	M	F	Y
S	B	W	Q	I	M	I	N	I	B	F	S	E	C	L	A	R	N
E	A	R	V	Y	N	T	O	U	I	A	C	A	I	D	R	E	N
M	R	E	I	E	C	H	S	C	N	N	H	D	R	E	I	B	A
L	B	G	P	C	N	I	U	L	G	N	U	I	P	S	A	E	M
O	A	N	Q	S	E	L	N	I	S	Y	L	L	E	O	N	C	U
H	R	A	G	A	R	O	G	L	F	M	L	W	C	N	N	C	H
A	A	L	B	X	R	U	A	I	C	E	Y	H	N	J	A	A	C
T	S	U	R	T	A	M	M	B	W	N	N	C	E	E	M	C	S
S	T	O	A	D	F	Z	Z	O	E	D	S	A	R	N	A	L	A
U	R	B	B	C	E	G	P	U	R	E	T	E	O	N	R	A	R
G	O	A	U	C	S	A	R	L	D	L	R	B	L	Y	T	R	A
U	Z	I	X	E	I	R	I	A	N	S	O	Y	F	N	I	K	L
A	Z	D	Z	B	U	D	C	N	A	S	Z	M	E	N	N	E	C
D	I	A	O	G	O	H	L	G	M	O	D	A	P	A	E	Z	T
W	F	N	D	E	L	S	S	E	C	H	C	T	Y	M	S	Z	Y
H	E	F	O	X	L	G	E	R	U	N	O	L	F	U	G	U	A
Z	N	E	G	N	I	B	F	O	D	R	A	G	E	D	L	I	H

Amy Beach (1867–1944)

Her *Gaelic Symphony* was the first to be composed and published by an American woman.

Augusta Holmès (1847–1903)

Banned from studying music when she was a child, this French composer of Irish descent was only able to begin lessons after her mother died.

Barbara Strozzi (1619–77)

This Baroque singer and composer had more music in print than any of her peers throughout the era.

Clara Schumann (1819–96)

Recognise the surname? Yes, Clara Schumann was married to composer Robert, but she was also a marvellous composer in her own right and one of the finest pianists of the Romantic era.

Ethel Smyth (1858–1944)

Smyth wrote 'The March of the Women', the anthem of the women's suffrage movement. She was also the first female composer to be given a damehood.

Fanny Mendelssohn (1805–47)

Another familiar surname – Fanny Mendelssohn published a lot of her works under her brother Felix's name to avoid causing a stir.

Florence Price (1887–1953)

The first African-American woman to have her work performed by a national symphony orchestra.

Hildegard of Bingen (1098–1179)

A mystic, polymath and visionary abbess – and also the first named composer in the world. All composers before her remained anonymous.

Lili Boulanger (1893–1918)

This French composer was the first female winner of the Prix de Rome composition prize.

Louise Farrenc (1804–75)

In 1842, she became the only woman of the 19th century to be appointed as professor at the Conservatoire de Paris.

Marianna Martines (1744–1812)

Alongside Haydn and Mozart, Martines was also composing up a storm in Vienna.

Min Huifen (1945–2014)

The 'Queen of Erhu', a traditional Chinese stringed instrument, was not only an incredible musician but a talented composer, too.

Nadia Boulanger (1887–1979)

Lili's sister was also a composer but is best remembered as possibly the greatest music teacher ever. Her students include Philip Glass, Aaron Copland, Leonard Bernstein and Quincy Jones.

Rebecca Clarke (1886–1979)

Many of this violist's works have only recently been published, and the classical music world is realising what they've been missing.

Zenobia Powell Perry (1908–2004)

A professor, pianist, civil rights activist, prolific composer and friend of Eleanor Roosevelt, Perry didn't begin creating her own arrangements in earnest until she was in her forties.

8: False. Only two women have been nominated for more than 50 Grammys: Beyoncé and Dolly Parton. Beyoncé has been nominated 88 times, and has won 32 Grammys, making her the most awarded artist in the history of the awards. Dolly has been nominated 54 times, has won 10 Grammys.

9: Marni Nixon. At the time, her work went uncredited, but the scope of her contribution to movie musicals is now legendary throughout the industry. Not only were audiences kept in the dark, but sometimes even the actors she dubbed weren't told – when Marni sang the part of Maria in *West Side Story*, actress Natalie Wood had no idea her voice wouldn't be in the final movie.

10:

Lyric	Artist	Song Title	What Comes Next
Tumble outta bed and I stumble to the kitchen	Dolly Parton	'9 To 5'	Pour myself a cup of ambition
They paved paradise, and put up a parking lot	Joni Mitchell	'Big Yellow Taxi'	With a pink hotel, a boutique, and a swingin' hot spot
Summertime, and the living is easy	Ella Fitzgerald	'Summertime'	Fish are jumping, and the cotton is high
Birds flying high, you know how I feel	Nina Simone	'Feeling Good'	Sun in the sky, you know how I feel

| Lucky you were born that far away so | Shakira | 'Whenever, Wherever' | We could both make fun of distance |
| If you need me, call me | Diana Ross | 'Ain't No Mountain High Enough' | No matter where you are |

11:

'I Will Always Love You' by Whitney Houston – written by Dolly Parton

'Party In The U.S.A.' by Miley Cyrus – written by Jessie J

'Diamonds' by Rihanna – written by Sia

'Breakaway' by Kelly Clarkson – written by Avril Lavigne

'Till The World Ends' by Britney Spears – written by Kesha

'(You Make Me Feel Like) A Natural Woman' by Aretha Franklin – written by Carole King

Dolly Parton says she wrote 'I Will Always Love You' on the same day as 'Jolene'. Steady on, Dolls!

Jessie J wrote 'Party In The U.S.A.' for herself, but then decided not to record it. The royalties she received after Miley Cyrus released the song paid her rent for three years.

Sia wrote 'Diamonds' in 14 minutes. It became her first number one hit for another artist.

Avril Lavigne wrote 'Breakaway' for her first album, but it didn't make the cut. Her original demo version is still floating around the internet, however.

Kesha wrote 'Till The World Ends', and says that she's 'never been more proud of anything' in her career. She and Nicki Minaj join Britney Spears on the remix.

Carole King wrote '(You Make Me Feel Like) A Natural Woman' for Aretha Franklin with her first husband, Gerry Goffin. It was a smash hit, but then she *is* one of the most successful female songwriters of all time, writing 118 Billboard Hot 100 and 61 UK Singles Chart hits. Aretha, of course, was one of the greatest singers of all time, and in 1987 became the first woman to be inducted into the Rock & Roll Hall of Fame.

PHYSICAL EDUCATION

1: a) The Doha Pearl

After being told that her kidney stone was too big to do anything about before the championships, Simone Biles decided to soldier on regardless – despite pain medication being out of the question while competing.

2: Mattel made a Dina Asher-Smith Barbie.°

3: c) She won three track and field medals
Babe Zaharias took home gold in the 80-metre hurdles
and the javelin, silver in the high jump and set three
world records over the course of the event to boot.
She remains the only track and field athlete to win
individual Olympic medals in running, throwing *and*
jumping events. Babe was also brilliant at basketball
and baseball (she is still the world record holder for
the furthest baseball throw by a woman, set in 1931
with a distance of 296ft). Despite being a latecomer to
golf, she won 10 major Ladies Professional Golf Association championships throughout her short career, as
well as dozens of other golf titles. When she died at the
age of 45, she was still at the top of her golfing game.

4: a) Joined a convent
After more than a decade dancing at the Paris Opéra,
creating leading roles for female dancers in ballets that
had, until her debut in 1681, been danced solely by
men, Mademoiselle De Lafontaine swapped pirouettes
for prayers, and retired to a convent.

5: False. Fanny Blankers-Koen was actually 30 and had
two children, earning her the typically condescending

nickname of 'the flying housewife'. Her critics thought she should stay at home and look after her kids, which made her even more determined to prove them wrong. She was the most successful athlete at the Olympics that year.

6: In 1971 – 50 years after the Football Association decided it was an unsuitable sport for a woman (despite teams such as Dick, Kerr Ladies F.C. – pictured on page 108 – drawing crowds of 53,000 spectators in the aftermath of the First World War). The ban didn't stop women playing recreationally, but it did mean they couldn't take to the pitch at the larger grounds of FA-affiliated clubs.

7: b) The Football Association
In what was meant to be a heartwarming story about the Lionesses being reunited with their families after the World Cup, the (male) content editor at the Football Association scored an own goal when he enraged half of the internet.

8:

    a) Annie Oakley, who beat her future husband in an 1875 Thanksgiving sharpshooting competition.

b) Jackie Tonawanda, the boxer who took on Larry Rodania in Madison Square Garden – and won. She also fought the New York State Athletic Commission, taking them to court for the chance to get a licence to box professionally.

c) Fallon Sherrock, who became the first woman to defeat a man at the PDC World Darts Championship in 2019.

d) Ann Glanville, whose all-women rowing crew famously defeated 10 of the best male crews at a regatta in Le Havre in 1833.

e) Billie Jean King, the tennis champion and equality campaigner who triumphed over former male number one Bobby Riggs in 1973.

f) Madge Syers, the first woman to compete at the Ice Skating World Championships in 1902. She beat two men to win the silver medal.

9:

Gertrude Ederle	First woman to swim the Channel
Hélène de Pourtalès	First woman to win Olympic gold
Kathrine Switzer	First woman to officially run the Boston Marathon

Jasmin Paris	First woman to win the gruelling 268-mile Spine Race
Khadijah Mellah	First woman to ride at a major British racecourse wearing a hijab
Wilma Rudolph	First American woman to win three gold medals at a single Olympic Games

Gertrude Ederle swam the Channel in 1926 in terrible weather, and choppy seas meant she was forced off course and actually swam 35 miles instead of 21.

Sailor **Hélène de Pourtalès** won gold with the Swiss team at the 1900 Olympics. Two months later (in those days, the Olympics went on for a long, long time), English tennis ace Catherine Cooper became the first woman to win individual Olympic gold.

Kathrine Switzer ran the Boston Marathon in 1967, and was assaulted along the way by a volunteer official who clearly thought women didn't belong there. She has run it several times since then, including 50 years later, at the age of 70. In tribute to her barrier-breaking race, her number 261 will never be assigned to another runner. She was the race's first official female finisher, but the equally trailblazing Bobbi Gibb had run it the year before without a bib number to become the first woman to complete the Boston Marathon since it began in 1897.

Jasmin Paris not only won the Spine Race, but she shaved a cool 12 hours off the previous course record by completing it in 83 hours, 12 minutes and 23 seconds. Oh, and she had to stop along the way to express milk for her baby.

Khadijah Mellah was a teenager from Peckham when she shook up the horseracing world by wearing a hijab under her helmet, and, well, by simply being a teenager from Peckham. She joined the Ebony Horse Club in Brixton in 2012 and began racing in April 2019. Four months later, she won the Magnolia Cup (a charity race at Goodwood), despite being the youngest and most inexperienced rider there.

In the 1960s, **Wilma Rudolph** was the fastest woman in the world. She survived childhood pneumonia, scarlet fever and polio, and wore a brace on her weak left leg until she was 12, making her record-breaking three gold medals at the Rome Olympics all the more remarkable.

10: c) 2014
In 2014, a 260-year ban on women was overturned when members voted 85% in favour of shaking up its ridiculously outdated rules. Plans for an actual women's changing room weren't drawn up until five years later.

11:

ACT IT US – Catsuit

HORSTS – Shorts

BARK NIP – Pink bra

AH JIB – Hijab

In 2018, the French Tennis Federation deemed Serena Williams' choice of French Open outfit – a black catsuit – to be inappropriate, stating that it would be banned from future tournaments because 'one must respect the game and the place'.

The English Bowling Federation said men could wear shorts, but women couldn't. This was in 2019, by the way, not 1919.

Tennis got its (pristinely white) knickers in a twist when Venus Williams let her pink bra straps show on the opening day of the 2017 Wimbledon tournament. She changed her bra during a rain break, but wasn't up for a post-match chat about her underwear, saying: 'What pink bra? I don't like talking about bras in press conferences. It's weird.'

Muslim women were forced to choose between faith and football when FIFA banned the wearing of the hijab (and all head coverings) in 2007. It took seven years of campaigning by fearless players and supporters to get the ban lifted.

HISTORY

1: b) 8,000

Women made up over 75% of Bletchley's workforce – forming a total of 8,000 female employees. So secret was the work that they carried out, some employees didn't even know that they were code breaking. It wasn't until 1974 that the secrets of Bletchley Park could be openly talked about.

2:

From the outside, **Empress Elisabeth of Austria** (1837–1898) had a glamorous and charmed life, but in reality she was struggling with an absent husband, a domineering mother-in-law and grieving the loss of her second child. While travelling in Geneva she was assassinated by an anarchist who stabbed her in the heart.

Regarded as a woman of brilliant character and intelligence, Queen Consort of Great Britain **Caroline of Ansbach** (1683–1737) was a trusted advisor to King George II during their marriage, but she suffered serious health problems throughout her life, including gout and a hernia. She died after her strangulated bowel burst.

Lady Jane Grey (1537–54) was nominated to be queen by Edward VI, who named her in his will, bypassing his male heirs and Mary I. However, she was queen for just nine days. Support for Mary to become the rightful heir to the throne grew and Lady Jane Grey was eventually beheaded for high treason.

Egyptian queen **Cleopatra** (c.69 BCE–30 BCE) has been the source of many stories, but the one that's left historians questioning for centuries is exactly how she died. It's rumoured that she died by suicide with a venomous snake, a tale certainly worthy of a Shakespearean tragedy and an Elizabeth Taylor film. However, the earliest accounts of her death from Greek and Roman philosophers Strabo and Plutarch were compiled generations after her death. As poetic as the snake theory is, if she did choose a poison to end her life, she would have likely drunk it instead.

It was an ancient law in Thailand that forbade a civilian to touch a member of the royal family which led to the tragic death of **Sunanda Kumariratana** (1860–80). When the river boat she was on capsized, the queen drowned while her subjects stood helpless and watched.

There are many rumours about the way in which the Russian Empress **Catherine the Great** (1729–96) died, and the truth has nothing to do with her having sex with a horse. She had a stroke in the bathroom and died the following day.

Rani Lakshmi Bai (1828–58) was wounded in battle when leading the Indian rebellion against Britain. She dressed as a man to fight alongside her soldiers and refused to surrender even when her armies were vastly outnumbered.

Amalasuintha, ruler of the Ostrogoths (c. 495–535) held an influential position throughout her life as Queen Regent for her son. Alas, her choice in advisors proved questionable. She was imprisoned by her co-ruler (and cousin) Theodahad, and murdered in the bath.

Although **Joanna of Castile** (1479–1555) died of a fever, that's not the whole story. Her untimely end was due to the forced imprisonment by her son, Charles I, who did everything he could to keep her in confinement and ensure his power, even demanding that no one speak to her.

3: c) They were a gang of jewel thieves
The Forty Elephants were a terrifying group of jewel thieves that terrorised London shopkeepers. Founded

in the late 18th century by artist's model Mary Carr, the group's infamy was largely due to her successor, Alice Diamond. The well-dressed women hid their stolen loot under their bustles and large dresses.

4: c) 60,000

It's impossible to know the exact number of women who were executed, or indeed the methods used, but it is thought that approximately 60,000 were killed after being indicted as witches. Witches being burned at the stake may be a widely-held idea, but it was in fact a rare occurrence, although many of the bodies were burned after death. It's far more likely that these women were tortured or hanged, or both. Their crimes were often entirely fabricated; many accusations of witchcraft actually arose from disputes between neighbours, and poor, elderly women were frequently accused.

5:

C	E	R	R	O	R	H	W	J	D	B	S	E	C	N	D	F
P	A	D	U	X	D	X	E	N	R	E	A	W	Y	I	T	
C	V	T	G	O	H	U	C	G	A	I	T	X	K	E	E	H
A	O	F	H	P	M	R	S	N	V	H	B	K	H	L	D	G
T	U	I	J	E	O	Y	R	U	E	U	U	T	D	O	S	K
H	C	T	A	V	R	G	E	R	R	J	T	V	T	B	R	X
E	S	N	I	K	X	I	I	S	E	V	P	S	M	E	E	Y
R	D	D	E	Q	C	N	N	I	E	X	I	T	C	N	K	K
I	C	U	I	C	E	F	E	E	H	N	E	V	H	N	D	X
N	Y	H	M	P	F	J	D	Y	O	C	A	X	E	A	E	Y
E	W	Q	A	E	Y	G	L	A	S	F	L	J	V	D	F	G
H	O	R	N	I	M	F	R	U	V	N	A	D	T	E	B	B
O	R	B	E	H	E	A	D	E	D	O	C	R	K	T	E	H
W	V	S	Y	I	Z	Y	Q	M	D	P	P	E	A	Q	S	L
A	C	N	K	T	F	G	C	A	O	D	E	A	K	G	M	S
R	S	E	V	E	L	C	F	O	E	N	N	A	E	X	O	H
D	Q	N	P	F	B	P	K	S	V	T	Z	I	I	P	Y	N

Catherine of Aragon married Henry VIII (her late husband's brother) in 1509. When she didn't give birth to a son, he split from the Catholic Church so he could divorce her to marry. . .

. . . **Anne Boleyn** in secret in 1533. She had a daughter – Elizabeth – but she failed to produce a male heir and so Henry had her investigated for high treason (a common theme in kings wanting to get their own way). The investigation found her guilty of adultery, incest and conspiring against the king and she was beheaded at the Tower of London in 1536.

It's probably no surprise that Henry first showed interest in **Jane Seymour** some three months before Anne's death. Jane served both Catherine of Aragon and Anne and married the king at Hampton Court Palace in 1537. She was very formal and the French fashions at court that Anne favoured were quickly banned. She gave birth to a long-awaited son, but complications during childbirth meant she died only days later.

Two years later, Henry married **Anne of Cleves**, although marriage negotiations began soon after Jane's death. However, after just six months of wedded bliss, Henry had the marriage annulled, claiming it was never consummated. Ever the charmer, he blamed his advisors for lying about how pretty she was. She did at least get a very generous settlement, which included Richmond Palace and Hever Castle, and amazingly, the couple remained friends after the dissolution of their marriage.

By the time Henry married **Catherine Howard** in 1540 he was 49 and she was just 17. Their marriage took place less than three weeks after his annulment. A year into their marriage, Henry accused her of sleeping with her distant cousin, Thomas Culpeper, and she was executed.

Henry's final wife – **Catherine Parr** – survived him. After his death in 1547, Catherine took on the role as Elizabeth's guardian and lived the remainder of her life as Queen Dowager. She remarried six months after Henry's death but in 1548 she passed away after complications in childbirth.

6:

DARN HENNA HAT – Hannah Arendt

PARIAH CHIP – Hipparchia

WANNA DECAY ONLY – Lady Anne Conway

LOAF HIPPO PIT – Philippa Foot

LLAMA TYRES – Mary Astell

7:

a) True

Queen Victoria also ensured that no one else wore white to her wedding so as not to take the focus away from her (although it's hard to imagine anyone upstaging the actual queen). It's rumoured that the pattern for her gown – complete with 5.5 metre-long train – was destroyed so no one else could copy it.

b) True

There were actually eight attempts made to assassinate Queen Victoria and she was eventually given a parasol lined with chainmail to use as protection.

c) False

Queen Victoria was actually the first British monarch to take a train journey. She travelled from Slough to Paddington in 1842. While the queen continued to travel by rail throughout her reign, she was always concerned about speed, and the trains were only permitted to go at 40mph in daylight and even slower at night. They had to stop completely when she took meals, so you'd probably have been better off taking the bus.

8:

a) Sojourner Truth was born into slavery. When she escaped in 1826, she went to court for custody of her son, becoming the first black woman in the United States to sue a white man – and win. She continued fighting for the abolition of slavery – in 1851, she gave her best-known speech, 'Ain't I A Woman?'

b) Rosa Parks famously refused to give up her seat to a white passenger on a segregated bus in Montgomery, Alabama, in 1955 – a moment that launched the Montgomery Bus Boycott, one of the civil rights movement's pivotal campaigns.

c) Nine months before Rosa Parks, 15-year-old Claudette Colvin also refused to give up her seat on a Montgomery bus. She was arrested and was later a plaintiff in *Browder v Gayle*, the court case that ruled segregation on buses in Alabama was unconstitutional.

d) Elizabeth Eckford was one of the Little Rock Nine – a group of teenagers who navigated violent protesters on their first day at a previously all-white high school. They were admitted three years after the Supreme Court had ruled racial segregation in schools was illegal. Elizabeth was the first to arrive, and after the National Guard blocked her entrance, she had to flee the hundreds-strong crowd chanting, 'Two, four, six, eight, we ain't gonna integrate'. The black students were finally allowed to start school on 25 September 1957, but were subjected to physical and verbal abuse by their white classmates during their time there. Among the teens who made civil rights history as the Little Rock Nine were six girls: Elizabeth was joined by Carlotta Walls LaNier, Melba Pattillo Beals, Thelma Mothershed-Wair, Minnijean Brown-Trickey and Gloria Ray Karlmark.

e) Marian Anderson was one of the finest contraltos of her day. When she was banned from performing at Washington DC's Constitution Hall because she was black, First Lady Eleanor Roosevelt conspired with others to organise a bigger, better, and altogether more welcoming and less racist event for the singer. Marian sang for a crowd of 75,000 at the Lincoln Memorial on Easter Sunday in 1939.

f) Harriet Tubman escaped slavery and then helped rescue at least 70 enslaved people via the Underground Railroad, a secret network of safe houses, earning her the nickname 'Moses'.

9: c) White wine

Apparently, Mary, Queen of Scots used white wine to keep her complexion clear but it got very expensive for the Earl of Shrewsbury when she was in his custody. We don't recommend trying this at home with a bottle of Chardonnay, not least because you'll smell like the backend of your local wine bar. Mary wasn't the only queen to go to extreme lengths to keep her skin white. Nero's wife Poppaea reputedly opted for milk baths, and Elizabeth I preferred to slather on white make-up containing lead. Yes, regardless of what it did or didn't do for her face, it was incredibly poisonous.

10: a) In a toolbox
Irena and her fearless team used whatever they could to smuggle children out of the ghetto, including potato sacks and coffins. They trained a German Shepherd to bark when guards approached their van, to drown out the noise of children's cries. Elżbieta's mother hid a silver spoon engraved with her daughter's nickname – Elżunia – and her date of birth inside the carpenter's toolbox before she said goodbye.

11: King's Cross. Rumour has it that Boudicca may be buried somewhere below platform 8, 9 or 10. However, some think her grave is on Hampstead Heath, others believe she's buried at Stonehenge or in Norfolk, and more recently, archaeologists wondered if her final resting place might be under a McDonald's in Birmingham.

REPORT CARD

Add up your scores here to find out how well you have done:

SUBJECT	SCORE
Literature	/ 64
Geography	/ 39
Mathematics	/ 36
Drama	/ 55
Science	/ 63
Politics	/ 39
Art and Design	/ 59
Music	/ 58
Physical Education	/ 40
History	/ 43
OVERALL SCORE	____ / 496

TEACHER'S COMMENTS

0–170

GRADE: C

Has a tendency to daydream but shows occasional flashes of brilliance when prompted. Spends a lot of time shrieking 'I DIDN'T KNOW THAT!' and then forgets all newly acquired facts instantly. Top marks for enthusiasm, however – with further reading could be very knowledgeable.

171-326

GRADE: B

Displays a good understanding of some subjects, but can become distracted by making plans to topple the patriarchy. Finds the lure of going on strike in the name of feminism very appealing. Motivated by a desire to shut up mansplainers with astounding facts, which is a noble endeavour.

327-496

GRADE: A

A stellar student who has clearly undertaken a lot of extra study at home. On track to change the world, but not before calculating the gender pay gap of every industry, organising a mass protest, hosting a feminist book club and appearing on *Mastermind* with the rather broad specialist subject of 'Women'.

FURTHER READING

Inspired to discover more? Here are some books that will take your knowledge to the next level.

Literature

A Literature of Their Own: British Women Novelists from Brontë to Lessing by Elaine Showalter

A Room of One's Own by Virginia Woolf

A Vindication of the Rights of Woman by Mary Wollstonecraft

Jane Austen: A Life by Claire Tomalin

Changing My Mind by Zadie Smith

The Bitch Is Back: Wicked Women in Literature by Sarah Appleton Aguiar

The Brontës by Juliet Barker

The Life of Charlotte Brontë by Elizabeth Gaskell

Smile Please by Jean Rhys

Geography

And I'd Do It Again by Aimée Crocker

Around the World in Seventy-Two Days and Other Writings by Nellie Bly

The Blessings of a Good Thick Skirt: Women Travellers and Their World by Mary Russell

The View from the Ground by Martha Gellhorn

Unsuitable for Ladies: An Anthology of Women Travellers by Jane Robinson

Mathematics

Broad Band: The Untold Story of the Women Who Made the Internet by Claire L. Evans

Hidden Figures: The Untold Story of the African American Women Who Helped Win the Space Race by Margot Lee

Life in Code by Ellen Ullman

Power in Numbers: The Rebel Women of Mathematics by Talithia Williams

The Thrilling Adventures of Lovelace and Babbage: The (Mostly) True Story of the First Computer by Sydney Padua

Drama

Backwards and in Heels: The Past, Present and Future of Women Working in Film by Alicia Malone

Mommie Dearest by Christina Crawford

Renegade Women in Film and TV by Elizabeth Weitzman

Scandals of Classic Hollywood: Sex, Deviance, and Drama from the Golden Age of American Cinema by Anne Helen Petersen

The Female Gaze: Essential Movies Made by Women by Alicia Malone

You Must Remember This – podcast by Karina Longworth

Science

Chrysalis: Maria Sibylla Merian and the Secrets of Metamorphosis by Kim Todd

Headstrong: 52 Women Who Changed Science – and the World by Rachel Swaby

Inferior: How Science Got Women Wrong – and the New Research That's Rewriting the Story by Angela Saini

No One Is Too Small to Make a Difference by Greta Thunberg

Rise of the Rocket Girls by Nathalia Holt

The Fossil Hunter: Dinosaurs, Evolution, and the Woman Whose Discoveries Changed the World by Shelley Emling

The Glass Universe by Dava Sobel

The Immortal Life of Henrietta Lacks by Rebecca Skloot

The Radium Girls by Kate Moore

Politics

Deeds Not Words: The Story of Women's Rights, Then and Now by Helen Pankhurst

From the Corner of the Oval by Beck Dorey-Stein

I Am Malala: The Story of the Girl Who Stood Up for Education and was Shot by the Taliban by Malala Yousafzai

Rise Up Women!: The Remarkable Lives of the Suffragettes by Diane Atkinson

Ruth Bader Ginsburg: A Life by Jane Sherron de Hart

Sophia: Princess, Suffragette, Revolutionary by Anita Anand

The Firebrand and the First Lady by Patricia Bell-Scott

We Should All Be Feminists by Chimamanda Ngozi Adichie

Art and Design

Breaking Ground: Architecture by Women by Jane Hall

Invisible Women: Exposing Data Bias in a World Designed for Men by Caroline Criado Perez

Leave Me Alone with the Recipes: The Life, Art, and Cookbook of Cipe Pineles edited by Sarah Rich, Wendy MacNaughton, Maria Popova and Debbie Millman

Magnificent Women and their Revolutionary Machines by Henrietta Heald

Women in Design: From Aino Aalto to Eva Zeisel by Charlotte Fiell and Clementine Fiell

Women in Design by Charlotte Fiell and Clementine Fiell

Broad Strokes: 15 Women Who Made Art and Made History (In That Order) by Bridget Quinn

Frida: The Biography of Frida Kahlo by Hayden Herrera

Lee Krasner: A Biography by Gail Levin

Ninth Street Women by Mary Gabriel

Stone Mirrors: The Sculpture and Silence of Edmonia Lewis by Jeannine Atkins

The Militant Muse: Love, War and the Women of Surrealism by Whitney Chadwick

Music

Bedsit Disco Queen by Tracey Thorn

Beyoncé in Formation: Remixing Black Feminism by Omise'eke Tinsley

Clothes, Clothes, Clothes. Music, Music, Music. Boys, Boys, Boys by Viv Albertine

Girl in a Band: A Memoir by Kim Gordon

Girls to the Front: The True Story of the Riot Grrrl Revolution by Sara Marcus

Hunger Makes Me a Modern Girl: A Memoir by Carrie Brownstein

I Could Have Sung All Night by Marni Nixon

I'm Not with the Band: A Writer's Life Lost in Music by Sylvia Patterson

Women in Jazz: The Women, The Legends & Their Fight by Sammy Stein

Physical Education

Fire on the Track: Betty Robinson and the Triumph of the Early Olympic Women by Roseanne Montillo

Game Changers: The Unsung Heroines of Sports History by Molly Schiot

Life in Motion: An Unlikely Ballerina by Misty Copeland

Little Girls in Pretty Boxes: The Making and Breaking of Elite Gymnasts and Figure Skaters by Joan Ryan

The Million Dollar Mermaid by Esther Williams

History

Her Brilliant Career: Ten Extraordinary Women of the Fifties by Rachel Cooke

The Diary of a Young Girl by Anne Frank

The Warrior Queens by Antonia Fraser

She-Wolves: The Women Who Ruled England Before Elizabeth by Helen Castor

Who Cooked the Last Supper: The Women's History of the World by Rosalind Miles

Women & Power: A Manifesto by Mary Beard

Women of Means: The Fascinating Biographies of Royals, Heiresses, Eccentrics and Other Poor Little Rich Girls by Marlene Wagman-Geller

Fiction

American Wife by Curtis Sittenfeld

Enchantress of Numbers by Jennifer Chiaverini

Finding Dorothy by Elizabeth Letts

I, Tituba, Black Witch of Salem by Maryse Condé

In the Time of the Butterflies by Julia Alvarez

Jubilee by Margaret Walker

Leonora by Elena Poniatowska

Miss Austen by Gill Hornby

Mrs Hemingway by Naomi Wood

Swan Song by Kelleigh Greenberg-Jephcott

Terrible Virtue by Ellen Feldman

The Aviator's Wife by Melanie Benjamin

The Chaperone by Laura Moriarty

The Dream Lover by Elizabeth Berg

The Gilded Years by Karin Tanabe

The Lacuna by Barbara Kingsolver

The Other Boleyn Girl by Philippa Gregory

The Paris Wife by Paula McLain

Vanessa and Her Sister by Priya Parmar

White Houses by Amy Bloom

Z: A Novel of Zelda Fitzgerald by Therese Anne Fowler

ACKNOWLEDGEMENTS

A huge thank you to everyone at Bonnier Books UK including:

Madiya Altaf – Editorial
Beth Eynon – Editorial
Joanna de Vries – Copy Editor
Jane Donovan – Proofreader
Sophie McDonnell – Design
Ella Holden – Production
Jenna Petts – PR
Ali Nazari – Marketing
Jessica Tackie – Marketing

IMAGE CREDITS

Mathematics

P.37 © agefotostock / Alamy Stock Photo.

Drama

P.46 © Everett Collection Inc / Alamy Stock Photo, **p.49** © cineclassico / Alamy Stock Photo, ScreenProd / Photononstop / Alamy Stock Photo, **p.50** © Everett Collection Inc / Alamy Stock Photo, **p.51** © Everett Collection Inc / Alamy Stock Photo, © Moviestore Collection Ltd / Alamy Stock Photo.

Politics

P.71 © Trinity Mirror / Mirrorpix / Alamy Stock Photo, © Graham Wood / Stringer / Getty Images, **p.72** © Pictorial Press Ltd/ Alamy Stock Photo, **p.73** © Science History Images / Alamy Stock Photo, © Trinity Mirror / Mirrorpix / Alamy Stock Photo.

Art and Design

p. 84 © Andreas von Einsiedel / Alamy Stock Photo, **p. 85** © Robin & Lucienne Day Foundation, **p.86** © The Josef and Anni Albers Foundation / Artists Rights Society (ARS), New York and DACS, London 2020, **p.87** © 2020. Cooper-Hewitt, Smithsonian Design Museum / Art Resource, NY / Scala, Florence.

Physical Education

P.108 © Ullstein bild Dtl. / Getty Images, **p.110** © Keystone / Getty Images, **p.111** © Trinity Mirror / Mirrorpix / Alamy Stock Photo, © Alex Davidson / Stringer / Getty Images, **p.113** © PA Images / Alamy Stock Photo, **p.114** © Ullstein bild Dtl. / Getty Images.

History

P.124 © Granger Historical Picture Archive / Alamy Stock Photo, **p.125** © PictureLux / The Hollywood Archive / Alamy Stock Photo, **p.126** © Archive PL / Alamy Stock Photo, **p.127** © Bettmann / Getty Images, **p.128** © Hulton Archive / Stringer / Getty Images, **p.129** © Alpha Historica / Alamy Stock Photos.